EDGE COMPUTING

Advances in Industry 4.0 and Machine Learning
Series Editor: M. Niranjanamurthy

Industry 4.0 refers to the industrial revolution that focuses heavily on interconnectivity, automation, machine learning, and real-time data. It involves automation and data exchange in manufacturing technologies and processes which include cyber-physical systems (CPS), the Internet of Things, Industrial Internet of Things (IIOT), cloud computing, cognitive computing, and artificial intelligence. The revolution of Industry 4.0 is giving manufacturers faster, more flexible, and more efficient processes to produce higher quality goods and at lower costs. Machine learning is the process of using software engineering principles, and analytical and data science knowledge, and combining both of those in order to take an ML model that is created and making it available for use by the product or the consumers. Aimed at senior undergraduate students, graduate students, and professionals, the proposed series will focus on discussing advanced concepts of Industry 4.0 and Machine Learning. Some of the emerging application areas include manufacturing processes, industrial engineering, electronics and communication engineering, computer science and engineering, and electrical engineering.

Edge Computing
Fundamentals, Advances and Applications
K. Anitha Kumari, G. Sudha Sadasivam, D. Dharani, and M. Niranjanamurthy

For more information about this series, please visit: https://www.routledge.com/Advances-in-Industry-4.0-and-Machine-Learning/book-series/CRCAIIAML

EDGE COMPUTING
Fundamentals, Advances and Applications

K. Anitha Kumari
G. Sudha Sadasivam
D. Dharani
M. Niranjanamurthy

CRC Press
Taylor & Francis Group
Boca Raton London New York

CRC Press is an imprint of the
Taylor & Francis Group, an **informa** business

First edition published 2022
by CRC Press
6000 Broken Sound Parkway NW, Suite 300, Boca Raton, FL 33487-2742

and by CRC Press
2 Park Square, Milton Park, Abingdon, Oxon, OX14 4RN

© 2022 K. Anitha Kumari, G. Sudha Sadasivam, D. Dharani and M. Niranjanamurthy

First edition published by CRC Press 2022

CRC Press is an imprint of Taylor & Francis Group, LLC

Library of Congress Cataloging-in-Publication Data

Names: Kumari, K. Anitha, author. I Sadasivam, G. Sudha, author. I Dharani, D., author. I Niranjanamurthy, M., author.
Title: Edge computing : fundamentals, advances and applications / K. Anitha Kumari, G. Sudha Sadasivam, D. Dharani, M. Niranjanamurthy.
Description: First edition. I Boca Raton, FL : CRC Press, 2022. I Series: Advances in industry 4.0 and machine learning I Includes bibliographical references and index. I Summary: "This reference text presents the state-of-the-art in edge computing, its primitives, devices and simulators, applications, and healthcare-based case studies. The text provides integration of blockchain with edge computing systems and integration of edge with Internet of Things (IoT) and cloud computing. It will facilitate the readers to setup edge-based environment and work with edge analytics. It covers important topics including cluster computing, fog computing, networking architecture, edge computing simulators, edge analytics, privacy-preserving schemes, edge computing with blockchain, autonomous vehicles, and cross-domain authentication. Aimed at senior undergraduate, graduate students and professionals in the fields of electrical engineering, electronics engineering, computer science, and information technology, this text: Discusses edge data storage security with case studies and blockchain integration with edge computing system. Covers theoretical methods with the help of applications, use cases, case studies, and examples. Provides healthcare real-time case studies are elaborated in detailed by utilizing the virtues of homomorphic encryption. Discusses real-time interfaces, devices, and simulators in detail"– Provided by publisher.
Identifiers: LCCN 2021027968 (print) I LCCN 2021027969 (ebook) I ISBN 9781032126081 (hardback) I ISBN 9781003230946 (ebook)
Subjects: LCSH: Edge computing.
Classification: LCC QA76.583 .K86 2022 (print) I LCC QA76.583 (ebook) I DDC 005.75/8–dc23
LC record available at https://lccn.loc.gov/2021027968
LC ebook record available at https://lccn.loc.gov/2021027969

ISBN: 978-1-032-12608-1 (hbk)
ISBN: 978-1-032-13821-3 (pbk)
ISBN: 978-1-003-23094-6 (ebk)

DOI: 10.1201/9781003230946

Typeset in Times
by MPS Limited, Dehradun

Dedication

Dedicated to
My parents, my husband, and my daughters B.A. Sudhiksha and
B.A. Visruthaa
– Dr. K. Anitha Kumari
My parents, my husband, and my sons S. Akilesh and S. Hemannth
– Dr. G. Sudha Sadasivam
My mother, my husband, and my daughter K. Aaradhyaa
– Ms. D. Dharani
My parents for their constant encouragement and blessings
– Dr. M. Niranjanamurthy

Contents

Preface

The most significant aspect of any product or application is its response time. Smart products and applications always come along with connected devices such as the Internet of Things (IoT). The immense usage of IoT devices in recent applications generates vast data which are used further to predict the future aspects, to prevent damages to the system, to detect flaws earlier, to enhance the business productions, to improve the quality of the system, and to satisfy customer expectations. Consequently, the generation of data will never be treated as useless. By considering the pace and quantity of generated data, the cloud platform is the broadly accepted medium for processing it. But the major unexpected inconvenience while using cloud platform is the downtime. As the cloud platform and its functionalities fully depends on Internet, the services may get interrupted unpredictably any time which leads to delayed response. Hence, the time-sensitive applications which require on-time decision-making might suffer accordingly. Edge computing comes up with a solution where the processing is done either on premises or near the source of the data. The edge devices placed on the source would process the data as and when it is generated so as to provide better services. This process minimizes the data pushed on to the cloud for processing. The real-time data analytics can also be applied on voluminous data directly on to the edge devices. In order to preserve the confidentiality and integrity of the data, several security mechanisms can also be applied on to the edge devices.

About the Book

The book *Edge Computing: Fundamentals, Advances and Applications* disseminates knowledge on edge computing gathered from industrial and academic experts for undergraduate and postgraduate students of Computer Science and Engineering, Information Technology and related disciplines as well as to related research scholars. The contents of the book have been delivered in a simple language and in a straightforward manner with suitable use cases. This book aims to balance between theory and practice of edge computing and its related concepts. The reader need not have prior knowledge of any specific concepts to understand the topics covered in this book. The explanations for the topics had been given with illustrations, examples, architectures, and code implementations wherever required. The book is organized into six chapters. They are Computing Paradigms, Edge Computing and Its Essentials, Edge Analytics, Edge Data Storage Security, Blockchain and Edge Computing Systems, and Edge Computing Use Cases and Case Studies.

Features of the Book

The following are the salient features of the book:

- Easy to understand
- Chapter outlines are listed at the start of each chapter
- Gathered the knowledge of Industry and Academic experts
- Results of demonstration for various topics are included
- Research challenges and future research directions are listed at the end of each chapter
- Imperative aspects are summarized at the end of each chapter
- References are listed at the end of each chapter

Organization of the Book

1. **Computing Paradigms:** The evolution of computing paradigms is elaborated in detail in this chapter. A detailed working nature is provided for parallel computing, distributed computing, grid computing, cloud computing, and mobile cloud computing by analyzing the pros and cons. The later part of the chapter covers the rise of fog computing/edge computing and osmotic computing. The chapter ends with current research issues.

2. **Edge Computing and Its Essentials:** The necessity of edge computing for real-time applications and streaming of data across the devices is illustrated in this chapter. Edge computing architecture, network management, and middleware required are elaborated. Architecture of IoTEdge-Sim, iFogSim, and EdgeSim simulators is illustrated to evaluate the various strategies and algorithms in a repeatable, controlled, and cost-effective way.

3. **Edge Analytics:** This chapter introduces the readers the fundamentals of data analytics and its approaches. Various phases and types of data analytics have been covered with examples and illustrations. The architecture of edge data analytics has been depicted and explained. Incorporation of general data analytics approaches to the edge devices are proposed. Included case studies and various programming tools and techniques related to edge analytics.

4. **Edge Data Storage Security:** Edge Data storage security schemes are discussed in detail with this chapter, namely, data confidentiality schemes, authentication schemes, and privacy-preserving schemes. The chapter mainly focuses on advanced encryption schemes like homomorphic encryption, attribute-based encryption, proxy re-encryption, functional encryption, and honey encryption. At the end of this chapter, attack detection and prevention strategies and possible research directions are included.

5. **Blockchain and Edge Computing Systems:** The security issues with edge computing systems are addressed by introducing blockchain technology. The concepts about blockchain and its components have been clearly explained from the beginning in such a way that the layman can understand the content. Characteristics, types, architecture, and essential blockchain fundamentals have been covered with neat illustrations. Various platforms and their working methodology have been covered with few practical demonstrations and code snippets.

6. **Edge Computing Use Cases and Case Studies:** High potential use cases of edge computing are elaborated in this chapter for better understanding by the research community. Three case studies are discussed in this chapter based on healthcare edge computing storage security. Open research challenges are added at the end for future research directions. An expert view is also added at the end of this chapter with few use cases to know about end-to-end Industrial IOT Products & Solutions from sensors to analytics.

Acknowledgments

We bow our head before "The God Almighty" who blessed us with health and confidence to undertake and complete the book successfully. We express our sincere thanks to the Principal and management of PSG College of Technology, for their constant encouragement and support. We thank our family who always stood beside us and encouraged us to complete the book by sharing our routine domestic chores. We are thankful to everybody who has motivated and guided us in preparing this book. A special thanks to the editorial team and the reviewers of CRC Press | Taylor & Francis Group for spending their valuable time and support in rapid publication of this book.

We would like to extend our gratitude to the various industry experts for providing their valuable expert notes for corresponding chapters. We would like to thank Mr. T. Viswanathan, CTO, Maxbyte Technologies, India and Dr. C.S. Saravana Kumar, Software Architect, Robert Bosch, India for providing valuable inputs on edge computing use cases and edge data analytics based on industry requirements. Also, we would like to thank Dr. Bithin Alangot, Researcher at Singapore University of Technology and Design for providing inputs on blockchain technology and its industry-related aspects.

We would like to thank the students Ananya M, Indusha M, Tharani RS, Sangavi GM, Aishwarya S, Lavanya N, Meshach P, Aswath Srimari R, Balaji R, and Vishnuvardhan S of the Department of Information Technology, PSG College of Technology for their valuable contribution in Ethereum Blockchain Implementation and realizing case studies in Edge Healthcare.

Dr. K. Anitha Kumari
Dr. G. Sudha Sadasivam
Ms. D. Dharani
Dr. M. Niranjanamurthy

Author Biographies

Dr. K. Anitha Kumari is working as an Associate Professor in the Department of IT for the past 11+ Years in PSG College of Technology, India. She is highly passionate and curious about learning new stuff in New Generation Computing Technologies. As an Independent Researcher, she had an opportunity to present her UGC-sponsored research paper based on Quantum Cryptography in the USA and visited a few foreign universities. To her credit, she had published a Patent and 75 Technical Papers in refereed and Impact Factored International/National Journals/Conferences published by IEEE, Elsevier, Springer, T&F, etc. Out of her research interest, she has contributed several book chapters published by CRC Press, Springer, IGI Global, etc. Currently, she's being the Program Coordinator of ME (Biometrics and Cyber Security) program and coordinated PSG CARE Sponsored One-Year Certification Course on Cyber Security (January–December 2020). She is also serving as anEditorial Member for Scopus-indexed/Open-access journals like *International Journal of Education, Science, Technology, and Engineering*, *International Journal of Artificial Intelligence, Decision Making: Applications in Management and Engineering*, etc., and acting as SPOC for the MoU signed between PSG and SETS Laboratory, Chennai. Also, she's been an Active Reviewer for prestigious journals published by IEEE (*IEEE Communications Surveys and Tutorials* [IF: 20.230], *IEEE Transactions on Industrial Informatics* [IF: 5.43]), IEEE Access, Springer, Wiley, etc., and Technical Program Committee (TPC) for many international/national conferences. Her areas of interest include Cloud & IoT Security, Design and Analysis of Security Protocols, Attacks & Defense, Security in Computing, Bioinformatics, Quantum Cryptography, Web Service Security, Network Security, Cognitive Security, and Analysis of Algorithms. She delivered ample Guest Lectures in her area of interest. Her security project is sanctioned and granted by AICTE for a sum of Rs.11,80,000. She's been the mentor for Technovator Projects (2019, 2018, and 2014) and "MEDROIDZ", an ICICI – Trinity 2014 funded project that was selected as one among the six projects in India. Academically, she has secured RANK-I and was awarded Gold Medal in ME (SE) and in BE (CSE) from Anna University and from Avinashilingam University. As a Supervisor, she is currently guiding Ph.D. scholars in her research area.

Dr. G. Sudha Sadasivam is working as a Professor and Heading the Department of CSE at PSG College of Technology. She has 24 years of teaching experience. She has published 5 books and around 100 papers in indexed journals. She has coordinated two AICTE-RPS projects and a UGC-sponsored project in the areas of distributed computing. She is the coordinator of PSG-Yahoo research in grid and cloud computing, Nokia Research on Personalization, Xurmo Research in social networking, and Cloudera project on VM migration in federated Cloud Environment. Her team has set up PSG-Yahoo/Nokia lab on Big Data Analytics at PSG College of

Technology. Her areas of interest include Distributed Computing and Big Data Analytics.

Ms. D. Dharani is working as an Assistant Professor in the Department of IT, PSG College of Technology, India. She received her M.Tech degree in Information Technology in 2016 and B.Tech degree in Information Technology in 2014 from Anna University, Chennai, and is currently pursuing Ph.D. in Information and Communication Technology from Anna University, Chennai. She had published several papers in International/National Journals/Conferences. She had also co-authored a book chapter entitled "COVID-19: AI-Enabled Social Distancing Detector Using CNN" and has been published by Springer. She had completed PSG CARE Sponsored One-Year Certification Course on Data Science. She had successfully completed NPTEL and Coursera certification courses on Blockchain. Her research interest includes areas of Blockchain Technology, Edge Data Analytics, and Machine Learning.

Dr. M. Niranjanamurthy is working as an Assistant Professor in the Department of Computer Applications, M. S. Ramaiah Institute of Technology, Bangalore, Karnataka. He is having 12* years of teaching experience and 2 years of industry experience as a Software Engineer. He has published six books in Scholars Press Germany, Wiley-SP, Springer and around 70* research articles in various International Conferences and International Journals. To his credit, he filed 18 Patents in that 3 were granted. He's being a Research Supervisor for four Ph.D. scholars in the area of Data Science, ML, and Networking. He is working as a reviewer in 22 International Journals, and two times got Best Research Journal Reviewer Award. He got a researcher award – Computer Science Engineering – 2018, 2019, 2020. He worked as a National/International Ph.D. examiner. He conducted various National and International Conferences, National Level Workshops, and Delivered Lectures. He is associated with various professional bodies like IEEE Member, Life Membership of "International Association of Engineers" (IAENG), Membership of "Computer Science Teachers Association" (CSTA). His areas of interest are Data Science, ML, E-Commerce, and M-Commerce related to Industry Internal Tool Enhancement, Software Testing, Software Engineering, Web Services, Web-Technologies, Cloud Computing, Big Data Analytics, and Networking.

1 Computing Paradigms

1.1 INTRODUCTION TO COMPUTING

One of the astounding scientific developments of humanity is the Computer. The word comes from the Latin word "Computare" that consists of two parts – "Com" meaning "together" and "putare" meaning "To settle (an account)". Computers are the devices used for computing. "Computing" is drawn from the Latin word "Computatio" that means reckoning or calculation. The process of computing uses computer technologies to complete a task. The process of *Computing* includes activities performed using computational devices to manage, process, and communicate information.

We have moved from the era where computers were considered as a luxury to an era where it is considered as necessity. We use some form of computing in our daily life without much ado. Using a cell phone, washing machine, communicating using email, financial transactions all include some form of computing. Task automation triggered using computers increases accuracy while reducing manual work, power, cost, and time. As quoted by the Association of Computing Machinery (ACM) [1], "Computing and computer technology are part of just about everything that touches our lives from the cars we drive, to the movies we watch, to the ways businesses and governments deal with us". Computing drives the innovations behind various fields like sciences, engineering, business, entertainment, and education.

The urge of humanity to make a device capable of solving complex problems between 1600 AD and 1800 AD leads to the invention of mechanical calculators. Blaise Pascal invented the first mechanical calculator in 1942. In 1671, Gottfried Wilhelm von Leibniz, the German mathematician designed the mechanical calculating machine called the Step Reckoner based on Pascal's invention. World War II saw the rise of electro-mechanical hybrid calculators. The first calculating computer Electronic Numerical Integrator and Computer (ENIAC) was completed after the war in 1946. It was basically designed during the war to handle complex calculations connected with the movement and strategies for the military during the war. Many scientists, mathematicians, and computer technicians worked hard to make the modern computer a reality. The computational capacity represented by the speed of the computers doubled every 1.5 years between 1975 and 2009. Beyond this sequential computing gave way to parallelism. Details are given in Section 3.

The growth of Internet, digital devices, and computer technology is the backbone behind a number of disruptive revolutionary business innovations like video streaming, mobile applications, retail medical clinics, Uber, Swiggy, digital cameras, and online education. In this digital age, computing has infiltrated into a number of domains as given in the following section.

DOI: 10.1201/9781003230946-1   1

1.2   THE MAJOR IMPACTS OF COMPUTING

Technologies that trigger innovations ensure the liveliness of a society. Bright and ethical technologists are the driving force behind the usage of computing for the benefit of the society. Today computing is an essential tool for every business, banking, government, entertainment, industry, education, and administration. It can be said of all large organizations, whether the department government or private, use a computer for a variety of their daily business and it is the fastest-growing industry in the world today [2].

- **Business**: Businesses use computers for a variety of purposes. Computing can be used to analyze current business trends, predict sales of a product, identify inventory, predict target customers, calculate salary, issue/receive orders, communicate business letters, create invoices, and more. They are also an essential tool for office automation that includes create/edit reports/documents, visualize sales, create presentations, manage business data, and more. Internet has fostered the growth of E-commerce industry.
- **Finance and banks**: Computing has fostered the growth of cashless society. The use of computers provides effective, fair, and personalized banking solutions. It can be used for maintaining accounts, managing investments, analyze profitability, and hence aid in reducing the operational budget of banks.
- **Industries**: Computers are used extensively to control and monitor the production process in various industries. This includes management of employee/customer information, maintaining and analyzing production and sales information, scheduling production, and so on.
- **Healthcare**: In the field of medical science, computers are used extensively to manage patient details, schedule appointments, administer purchase and inventory of medicines/equipment, aid in disease diagnosis, and for medical research. Advancements in the computing field have enabled the blind to see, the deaf to hear, the dumb to communicate, improvise learning, administer medicines among a few.
- **Home**: Smart home systems using microcomputers enhance home security and enable users to control various devices like air-conditioners, lights, televisions remotely. Online shopping and bill payment systems simplify various tasks. Spare time can be used for other purposes. Computers also help in budget planning and maintaining inventory. Children can use online learning resources to their benefit. Thus computers have turned into machines to maintain, manage, and communicate information in this modern world.
- **Education**: Computer technology can change the way we learn. Blended learning that combines classroom learning with online resources can enable students to understand the concept better. The use of videos, streaming, and augmented reality demonstrate a concept with animations and hence improves the learning of the student. Virtual classrooms can improve interactions. Teachers and management can use computers to store, maintain, and analyze student information. State of art distributed ledgers like blockchains help to

maintain student information in a secure manner. World Wide Web (WWW) is a huge repository of information. Computers facilitate students to search and access information from this huge repository. Computers aid in student registration, class scheduling, processing of examination results.

- **Law**: Computers are used extensively to gain access to information and for documentation. Intelligent systems can be also used for aiding lawyers for diagnostic and decision-making purposes. It includes analyzing and processing information to generate weekly and monthly reports, recording and maintaining payments, maintaining a legal information diary on court procedures with search facilities, maintaining a record of users.
- **Government sector**: uses the field of computing for effective administration and record keeping. Computing platforms can aid in effective storage/retrieval of data of citizens, services, projects, properties, organizations, and so on. It can be used for effective planning, communication, and decision-making. It can be used for traffic control, monitor enemy movement in borders, forecast weather, and predict disasters among a few.
- **Entertainment**: Computers are used extensively in various sports to predict and improve the performance of players, games, play music, drawing, and so on
- **Agriculture**: Computers are extensively used by farmers in the agricultural fields to record various soil and weather parameters and to automate various agricultural tasks. Various portals provide guides to farmers based on the daily conditions. Yield prediction, weather forecasts extensively rely on computing.

Rapid development of science and technology has changed the business systems in various domains. Manual tasks have been automated using computers. This reduces risks and improves effectiveness of the business systems in various domains including financial, industry, education, and administration. To conclude computers have become the brain behind the society.

1.3 PARALLEL COMPUTING

Since 1960, the fundamental components of a computer as described by the traditional Von Neuman Architecture consist of the memory, central processing unit, and the arithmetic unit and logical unit. Moore's law states that the transistor density doubles every 1.5 years. This in turn doubles the processing power. But this also reduces the space between the components and increases the power dissipation. This is because power dissipation increases by square of increase in clock speed. On an average, processor performance is increased by 52% every year between 1986 and 2002. After 2002, the performance stabilized. Clock speed could not be increased further due to power dissipation. Moore's law on increasing transistor density continues but clock speed has to be stabilized. This resulted in the emergence of a parallel computing paradigm using multiple cores. Here instead of increasing transistor density in a chip to improve performance of one processor, those transistors can be used to pack multiple processors into the same chip. Thus sequential computing gave way to parallelism.

Consider the case of solving a puzzle. Initially, pieces can be grouped as in Fig. 1.1. If only one person solves the puzzle, then maybe he takes 15 minutes. Consider two people are involved, then they solve their portion, communicate to solve the common portion and complete the work earlier, maybe in 9 minutes. On the other hand, if three people are involved, then they can solve it maybe in 6 minutes, but more communication is required. Multiple queues will speed up a service when compared to a single queue in contrast to multiple queues. An orchestra is an apt example for parallel processing where each instrumentalist does his work in a slot, maybe he may be in contention with another.

Parallel computing is the use of two or more processors (cores, computers) in combination to solve a single problem. Any problem is executed using a series of instructions. Consider that grades of ten students are to be calculated. Each student's record is processed by reading the marks, calculating the total, calculating the grade, and then printing the results. Let us consider that these form four instructions. So for ten students, 40 instructions have to be executed one after another on a single system. If each instruction consumes 1 unit of time, the total time consumed is 40 units. Now, if we have five processors, then grade of five students can be calculated in parallel. The problem is divided into five jobs with each job handling two students (Fig. 1.2). Hence for these five students as operations are done in parallel, it consumes only 4 units of time. Hence for ten students, it consumes 8 units of time. Hence performance is increased.

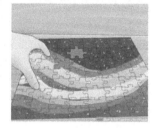

FIGURE 1.1 Puzzle and queue analogy to parallel processing.

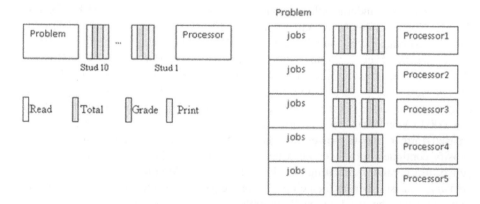

FIGURE 1.2 Sequential vs parallel processing – an example.

Parallel processing [3] can be done in instruction stream level or data stream level or both. When both instructions and data are processed sequentially it is called as single instruction stream single data (SISD) stream architecture. It is basically a serial computer. Data stream can be processed in parallel as in the figure above data of five students are processed in parallel. This architecture is called single instruction multiple data (SIMD) stream architecture. A set of instructions not dependent on one another can be processed in parallel. Such an architecture is called as multiple instruction single data (MISD) architecture. When multiple instructions each process different data, then it is multiple instruction multiple data (MIMD) architecture.

Some of the advantages of using parallel computing include:

- Parallel computing is highly suitable for modeling, simulating, and understanding complex, real-world phenomena. For example modeling road traffic which includes hundreds of vehicles and innumerable number of roads.
- Saves time as the job can be split into smaller tasks and executed in parallel.
- Reduces cost, as parallel systems can be constructed using cheap commodity computers.
- Complex problems like search, grand challenge problems require large computational power. This necessitates parallelization.
- Sharing of computational resources, for example, SETI@home project makes use of free processors for computation.
- Optimizing resource usage: As modern computers have multiple processors/ cores, using parallelization improves their utilization.

Communication between different processors in a parallel processing system can occur using a shared memory or a network [3].

1.3.1 SHARED MEMORY SYSTEMS

Here various processing units (P) share the same memory (M). All the communication between processors is through the shared memory. Based on whether the memory access time for all the processors is the same, shared memory systems are classified as uniform memory access (UMA) or non-uniform memory access (NUMA) systems (Fig. 1.3).

Such systems are fast. The main issue in this model is scalability. As all the processors communicate through the shared memory, it becomes a bottleneck. The architecture is tightly coupled as all communication is through the shared memory. Such shared memory systems are generally termed as parallel computing systems.

1.3.2 DISTRIBUTED MEMORY SYSTEMS

In these systems, each node has a processor (P) and memory (M). Each node is able to process independently. They communicate using networks. The network fabric is used for data transfer between nodes. Such systems are called as truly distributed systems (Fig. 1.4).

(a)   (b)

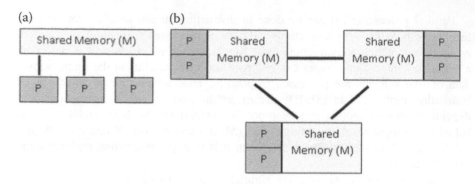

FIGURE 1.3 (a) Shared memory access (UMA) (b) non-uniform memory access (NUMA).

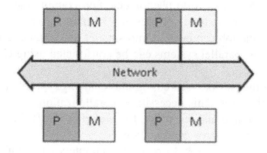

FIGURE 1.4 Distributed memory systems.

Such systems have higher scalability than shared memory systems as the interconnection network is only used for communication. It is fault-tolerant as another node can perform the functionality of the failed node. In case data is not available locally, it is fetched from another remote node. This results in non-uniform access time for remote data when compared to local data. Such systems are loosely coupled and can perform computation independently.

1.3.3 HYBRID MODEL

This model is a hybrid of shared memory and distributed memory architectures. The main advantage of this model is increased scalability like networked model. Further due to shared memory, access time is reduced (Fig. 1.5).

Thus parallel processing can be categorized from programmer's perspective as

- **Parallel processing**: when a single program is broken into independent tasks that can be executed in parallel.
- **Data parallelism**: when a large number of values are processed in parallel and the results are merged.
- **Multiprocessing**: wherein two or more independent programs are executed on separate processors.

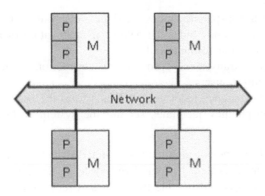

FIGURE 1.5 Hybrid systems.

Advances in networking and high-speed networks triggered to bloom of truly distributed systems.

1.4 DISTRIBUTED COMPUTING

The growth of networking technology with reduced data transfer latency and increased bandwidth was the driving force behind the emergence of distributed computing paradigm. The paradigm emerged with the initiation of communication between remote computing resources using message passing in the 1960s. The growth of local area networks, ARPANET, and email services in the 1970s triggered its growth. Distributed computing system is a system with multiple independent autonomous systems that communicate and coordinate actions in order to appear as a single coherent system to the end-user. When a job is given by the user, the system executes the job transparently. Users of the distributed system should be able to view the system as a virtual centralized system that is flexible, efficient, reliable, secure, and easy to use.

In a soccer team, each player has his own expertise and works autonomously. There is no shared state among players (no communication). Further, there is no global synchronization for player moves. The team has a common objective to defend the goal post and secure a goal. This is an apt analogy to a distributed system defined as "a collection of autonomous nodes communicating to address a problem collectively, with no shared memory and no common physical clock (for control)".

To meet this challenge, some of the factors to be considered in the design of the system [4,5] include:

- **Transparency:** This characteristic hides the details of the internals of the system from the user. Some of the types of transparencies include:
  - Location transparency: User is not aware of where the resource is located.
  - Migration transparency that hides the details as to whether a job has migrated from one node to another.

- Replication transparency hides the details of replicas from the user.
- Failure transparency hides the details of reallocation of another resource when a particular resource fails.
- Concurrency transparency provides an abstraction to sharing a resource among multiple users.
- Access transparency hides access details from the user.
- Scale transparency facilitates scaling the system without disrupting its services.

- **Reliability**: Existence of multiple nodes in a distributed system avoids single point of failure prevalent in centralized systems. To ensure reliability, distributed systems should be able to detect and recover from crash faults. In case of failure, suitable mechanisms to handle such failures should be designed to tolerate faults. To tolerate from faults, redundancy and decentralized control are frequently used. Redundancy is replicating the functionality/object in multiple nodes. This ensures that even if node fails, the functionality replicated in another node can be instantiated to make the system function. This offers the system capability to tolerate faults during its operation. Centralized control increases the possibility of single point of failure and hence reduces the reliability of the system. So decentralized control is preferred.
- **Fault detection and recovery**: Also enhance reliability of the system. It includes hardware and software mechanisms used to detect failures as well as mechanisms to correct the system state for continued operation. Atomic transactions, stateless servers, and use of acknowledgments for message transfers can increase system reliability.
- **Flexibility**: Facilitates introducing modifications in the system to meet the user needs. New functionalities or services can be added or existing services can be modified to make the system more effective and efficient.
- **Scalability**: Scalability refers to the capability of a system to adapt to increased service load. Decentralization helps to build scalable systems.
- **Security**: Resources in a distributed system should be protected against destruction and unauthorized access. Authentication and authorization can be provided using cryptography principles. Integrity of the messages and data should be preserved. Non-repudiation can be ensured using digital signatures. Security audits are essential.
- **Performance**: The performance of the distributed system should be better than that of a centralized system. Some of the measures taken to increase performance in distributed systems include employing fine-grain parallelism, minimizing the redundant copy operations and network traffic, batching the jobs before submission, and using caches to reduce data transfers/disk read/write operations.

Some of the advantages of distributed computing [6] include:

- **Performance**: As tasks in a distributed application can be executed in parallel by distributing the load across the nodes in the network, they yield good performance.

- **Collaboration:** Multiple applications can be connected through standard distributed computing mechanisms and communicate to complete their task collaboratively.
- **Higher reliability and availability:** As the applications/tasks are replicated across multiple machines, it offers better reliability.
- **Scalability:** Communication and loose coupling in distributed systems enable better scalability.
- **Extensibility:** Distributed applications can be dynamically reconfigured. Divide and conquer approach breaks up large problems into smaller ones, these individual components can be developed by smaller development teams in isolation.
- **Reuse:** The distributed components may perform various services that can potentially be used by multiple client applications. It saves repetitive development effort and improves interoperability between components.
- **Reduced cost:** Reuse and dynamic reconfiguration significant cost reductions can be achieved.

Hence in a truly distributed system or a peer-to-peer (P2P) system, the control is decentralized. In client-server architecture, the role of the client is to submit the job and the server completes the job and returns it to the client. In a P2P system, there is no difference between a client and a server node. For some tasks, a client can perform a server functionality. The system is self-organizing with distributed control without the need for centralized coordination by central server. P2P systems initially came into existence because of the need for file sharing (Fig. 1.6). The major advantages of a P2P system include:

- Work sharing
- Scalability
- Autonomy
- No single point of failure
- Reliability
- Cost reduction
- collaboration

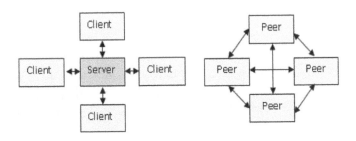

FIGURE 1.6 Client-server vs. P2P systems.

Security and trust management are complicated in a P2P environment when compared to the centralized client-server system. The system should be able to manage and maintain heterogeneous peers.

1.5 CLUSTER COMPUTING

Parallel processing systems achieve high performance but they are tightly coupled and costly. Such parallelism can also be achieved using a cluster of commodity systems. Clusters usually comprise homogeneous commodity hardware that is centrally controlled by a master server. The cluster operating system handles task distribution, monitoring, and collection transparently without user involvement. The operating system software shared by all the nodes in the cluster takes care of distributing the tasks and gathering results transparently without much involvement of the user.

Consider an orchestra that consists of a large group of musicians who play many different instruments together and are led by a conductor. An orchestra can be considered as an analogy for cluster computing (Fig. 1.7b). A cluster is a type of parallel or distributed processing system that consists of a collection of interconnected standalone computers that cooperatively work together as a single, integrated computing resource (analogous to various musical instruments). The major characteristic of a cluster is that nodes are homogenous and are centrally controlled by the master node (analogous to a conductor in an orchestra). The cluster operating system acts as a middleware to split the job into tasks and to communicate the tasks to the worker nodes. Once the worker nodes complete the tasks, the controller collects the results and informs the client. Hence the work is done transparently by the cluster. The cluster middleware offers a single system image (SSI) of the entire cluster to the user. Some of the components of a cluster include the following [4] (Fig. 1.7a):

1 Coordinator node to control the cluster.
2 Worker nodes that have their own resources such as processor, memory, and storage.
3 Network to provide communications between worker nodes and the coordinator node.
4 Gateway that acts as a firewall between the outside world and the cluster.

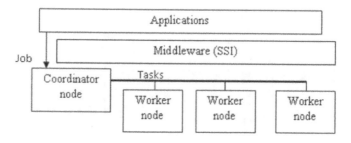

FIGURE 1.7A   Cluster architecture.

FIGURE 1.7B   Orchestra - An analogy to cluster.

When a cluster [7] is protected by a gateway, it is called as a closed cluster. When the cluster nodes can be freely accessed, it is called as an open gateway.

The following are some of the benefits of cluster computing:

1. Clusters are able to achieve a high performance-to-cost ratio when compared to mainframes. Cluster systems are made up of commodity hardware and are much cheaper than mainframes.
2. As a cluster has multiple nodes, tasks can be done in parallel. A cluster's performance is higher than an individual system and is comparable to that of a mainframe.
3. When compared to a mainframe, clusters have good fault tolerance. When a node in a cluster fails, its functionality is taken over by another node. This is not possible in a mainframe.
4. Cluster systems are scalable. It is easy to add a new node to the cluster without affecting the working of the other nodes.

Clusters offer two parallel programming models:

- Shared memory model, where all the processors share a common main memory and all communications can occur through the memory. This is a tightly coupled parallel processing system.
- Distributed memory model, where each node is provided with its own resources, including processors and memory, and the communication is through networks. This forms a loosely coupled distributed system.

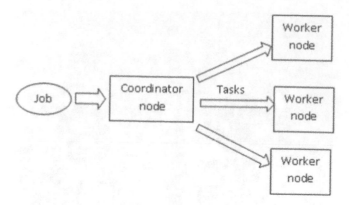

FIGURE 1.8 Parallel processing of tasks.

The basic goal of a cluster is to offer high performance by aggregating the power of various nodes, optimize the cluster efficiency by balancing the workload among different cluster nodes, and maintain redundancy to tolerate faults. Thus based on their functionality, clusters are categorized as follows.

1.5.1 High-Performance Clusters

When a job requires high computation, the job is split into smaller units called tasks and allocated to various nodes in the cluster. Resources like processors in the nodes will complete the tasks and return the results to the coordinator node. As the job is carried out in parallel by a number of nodes, it is completed quickly (Fig. 1.8).

1.5.2 Load Balancing Clusters

A load-balancing cluster assigns a task to the worker node that is least loaded. The load balancer has a monitor that continuously gets the resource utilization of the worker nodes. The coordinator node/controller receives the user's job, identifies the least loaded node using the load balancer, and allocates it to the least loaded worker (Fig. 1.9).

1.5.3 High-Availability Clusters

When critical jobs are executed in the cluster, and the worker node executing the job fails, the job cannot be completed. To tolerate such faults, the middleware takes care of allocating another node in the cluster to complete the job with minimum interruption. Such a cluster that is fault-tolerant is said to be highly available. To achieve high availability, the middleware should continuously monitor the availability of nodes using heartbeat messages. This can be centrally monitored by the coordinator node (Fig. 1.10).

Some of the limitations of clusters include effective resource utilization, single point of failure due to the controller node, and operating costs to maintain a cluster.

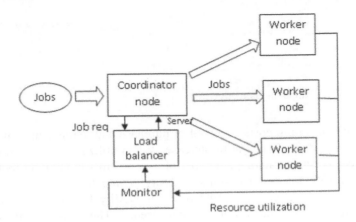

FIGURE 1.9 Load balancing.

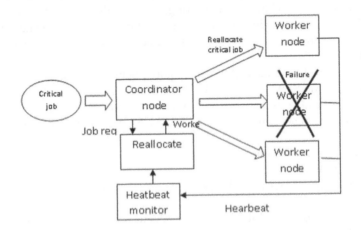

FIGURE 1.10 Fault tolerance.

Let us compare and contrast distributed computing with cluster computing. A cluster is a collection of tightly coupled independent computers with centralized control. These nodes work in cooperation to achieve a goal. Cluster systems are often kept in the same room. A distributed system consists of geographically dispersed independent computers that communicate using message passing in a loosely coupled environment. Parallel computation is possible in both these systems by harnessing the power of a large number of workstations. In reality, cluster computing is a special case of distributed computing with centralized control.

1.6 UTILITY COMPUTING

P2P and cluster architectures are technical models. They do not portray the service aspects of the computing industry. In a cluster model, the computing services are not utilized most of the time. Hence the system utilization is low.

FIGURE 1.11 Computing as a utility.

Further, the operating costs involved in purchase and maintenance of a cluster are high. To reduce costs and to increase system utilization, the computing resources can be shared among a number of users. Utility computing focuses on a business model, by which customers receive computing resources from paid service providers (Fig. 1.11). This offers flexibility for customers to request service providers for the resources when needed. The customers then pay the providers for the resources that they have utilized. Such a service provisioning business model is called as utility computing. Grid/cloud computing models fall under the umbrella of utility computing. This model maximizes the resource utilization and thereby reduces the operational costs. Just like water, electricity are offered as utility to individuals and businesses, computing is also offered as a utility.

A service-level agreement (SLA) is required between the service consumer and the provider. An SLA is a formal contract used to guarantee that the service provider will be able to meet the quality of service requirements of the consumer. This ensures customer satisfaction. A good SLA ensures the following:

- Customer satisfaction
- Quality of service
- Strengthen customer-service provider relationship

The architecture of the utility computing systems consists of the following layers (Fig. 1.12):

- User: is the entity that requests services of the provider through suitable applications.
- Service request examiner: interprets the QoS requirements from the service request of the customer and uses an admission control mechanism to decide whether to accept the request or not. It thus eliminates the requests from which resources are not available. It then triggers the SLA manager
- SLA manager: examines the SLA and discovers suitable service providers to satisfy QoS specified in the SLA. This entity is responsible for discovery, negotiation/renegotiation, pricing, scheduling, monitoring, SLA enforcement, dispatching, and accounting. The discovery component identifies the service provider who will be able to meet the QoS requirement of the requester. The pricing mechanism decides how service requests are to be charged. The SLA manager also schedules the requests to suitable providers from a list of providers who satisfy the agreement. The dispatching mechanism starts the execution of accepted service requests on allocated resources. The monitoring

FIGURE 1.12   SLA-oriented utility computing system architecture.

component periodically verifies whether QoS of requester is satisfied. If not, renegotiation is done. If SLA is violated it may result in termination of the contract or payment of penalties.
- Resource provider: is an entity which provides services to the customer in line with the SLA.

1.7   GRID COMPUTING

Cluster computing deals with homogenous systems that work cooperatively to complete a job. When we consider a real organization like a bank, it consists of a number of entities – computing devices, people, other devices like counting machines, applications customers. To automate an entire organization thus requires more than computers. This has led to the emergence of grid computing paradigm. The goal of a grid computing platform is to enable coordinated resource sharing and problem-solving in dynamic multi-domain virtual organizations.

Grid computing resources include computing power, data storage, hardware instruments, on-demand software, and applications.

Consider a group of physicists who want to study the ozone layer. The group requires devices to collect atmospheric data, mathematicians, physicists, computer scientists, computing devices, interfaces to complete their studies. All such connected heterogeneous entities form a grid (with data collection devices, computers, analytics software, mathematical modeling tools, interfaces). Heterogeneity and geographical distribution of resources in a grid environment necessitates the need for decentralized control (to enable better coordination) and open standards (for interoperability).

One of the most important concepts connected with grid computing [8] is a virtual organization. Grid computing aims at coordinated resource sharing among the participants in a virtual organization. For example, a physicist in California University uses dataset from the observation center in Italy. He analyses using a mathematical model formed by a mathematician in India using a simulation application. He then validates the result with observatory and stores the result at a storage provider. This virtual organization involves entities from at least four physical organizations – California lab, Italian Lab, Indian Lab, and service provider. It connects entities other than computing elements. The creation of such a virtual organization is based on the SLA between various physical entities. This includes the roles, activities, views, and administrative authorities of various members of the organization. All these entities form a huge grid to study Ozone (Fig. 1.13).

As in Fig. 1.14, one or more virtual organizations may share the same physical resources. Consider a VO for weather prediction. It requires resources for data collection, storage, analysis, and visualization of the result. This includes hardware resources like processor, hard disk, RAM, network along with software applications and frameworks. The hardware resources can be shared with another virtual organization (for financial domain).

Virtual organizations are thus

- Logical entities
- Dynamically created for a specific problem and thus have limited lifetime
- They can dynamically discover, provision, and manage the physical resources
- Entities can enter or leave the organization at any time
- Monitor the QoS specified in the SLAs
- Resource sharing is based on an open and well-defined set of interaction and access rules
- Sharing relationship among participants is peer-to-peer in nature

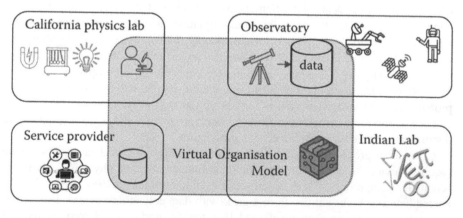

FIGURE 1.13   Virtual organizations.

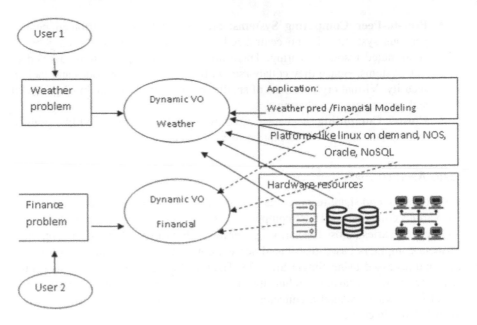

FIGURE 1.14   Resource sharing in virtual organization.

Grids can be basically classified as a computational or data grid. Scientific simulations like prime series, financial modeling does not involve a lot of data. But require lot of computation. These applications are computation-intensive. Processors and RAM are heavily used. Such a grid is said to be a computational grid. On the other hand, weather prediction and IoT require a lot of data to be analyzed. It requires heavy storage resources. Such grids are called as data grids.

Some examples of major business areas include:

- Genomic data analytics in the field of Life Sciences
- Predicting stock/product prices
- Research in data-intensive applications like IoT
- Automotive and aerospace engineering for design, modeling, and testing
- Enable seamless collaboration and flexibility among various government services
- Massively parallel, collaborative online games

The following paragraph compares Grid with related technologies.

- **World Wide Web**: The browser-server messaging model of WWW lacks complex interaction patterns needed to form a virtual organization.
- **Distributed Computing Systems**: There exist various distributed computing paradigms like CORBA, DCOM, RMI, etc. They lack interoperability and hence the capacity to form VO.

- **Peer-to-Peer Computing Systems**: are geographically distributed hetero-geneous systems with no centralized control. They complete their jobs by coordinated resource sharing. There are no virtual organizations defined in P2P systems. Hence they collaborate with large number of nodes and lack in security. Virtual organizations of smaller community facilitate more powerful and secure resource sharing.
- **Cluster Computing**: is characterized by centralized control and fine-grained parallelism. Hence VO cannot be formed effectively.

GRID ARCHITECTURE

To coordinate and share resources among the virtual organizations, the grid system has various components. These components comprised of the grid architecture. Grid architecture varies across the various generations. First generation of grid consisted of meta computers-based distributed servers connected via communication proto-cols and accessed using Single Sign-On. Then grid evolved based on Networking Architecture into a layered architecture in the second generation. Generation 3 is based on service-oriented architecture (SOA). This later evolved into a semantic Web 3.0 architecture.

Initially, grid computing started off with using free computational power in desktop systems as in SETI@HOME project. This is a form of volunteer computing or desktop computing. In volunteer computing, the client program runs on the volunteer's computer. It periodically contacts project servers over the Internet, asking for jobs and sending back the results of completed jobs. The goal of volunteer computing is to use the idle resources in desktop systems for research and scientific projects.

Some of the limitations of volunteer computing include:

- Availability of volunteers with needed resources to perform the task.
- Tasks performed on individual volunteer desktops should be independent with little / no communication between them.
- The success of volunteer computing depends on availability of volunteers to donate their free resources for computational purposes.
- Heterogeneity of hardware, operating systems, and applications of the vo-lunteer's systems.
- Trust of the volunteers ensures that the jobs are completed reliably without errors.
- Reliability can be enhanced using data and job replication techniques.

In Layered architecture, each layer provides services to the components in the layer above it. Various layers in bottom-up manner are as follows (Fig. 1.15):

- **Fabric layer:** comprises various resources including computational, storage, and cluster and network resources. Each resource has its own protocol to be followed.
- **Connectivity layer:** aims at establishing communication between various resources. TCP/IP stack is used for the same. Authenticity of the resources is decided using Single Sign-On related security protocols.

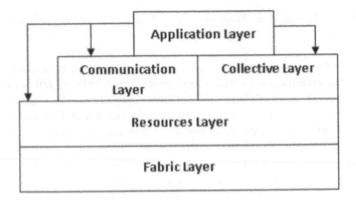

FIGURE 1.15 Layered grid architecture.

- **Resource layer:** protocols aim at coordination and sharing at the individual resource level. This layer monitors QoS of individual resources and maintains metadata of the resources like location, configuration, and usage of the resources.
- **Collective layer**: deals with a collection of resources. It offers services like resource discovery, scheduling, monitoring, and failure handling.
- **Application layer**: contains applications designed to make use of the various services of the underlying layers.

The major issue in layered architecture is a tight coupling of services offered by the layer. Each layer offers services to the layer immediately above it. In order to facilitate loose coupling between components, SOA can be used.

In SOA, software components offer services to various applications or other components. These services have used well-defined interfaces that expose a component's functionality. Thus application developers use the interfaces to interact with the component. The internal code of the component is not exposed to the developer. We can conclude that a service is user-facing software component of an application. Messages between the components and user are defined using standard protocols. Web service architecture is an instance of SOA. Open grid services architecture (OGSA) uses the functionalities in web services architecture (WSA) and defines a programming model using this emerging architecture. Services are loosely coupled peers that can singly or as a group can be composed or orchestrated to offer the capabilities of an application. OGSA is based on the core technologies of WSA:

- Extensible Markup Language (XML): to define the message exchange format and structure.
- Web Service Description Language (WSDL): is used to describe the interfaces of grid services.
- Simple Object Access Protocol (SOAP): defines message exchange patterns between grid/web components.

- Universal Description, Discovery, and Integration (UDDI): is used to discover services.

OGSA by the Global Grid Forum is an SOA that aims to define a common, standard, and open architecture for grid-based applications. "Open" refers to both the process to develop standards and the standards themselves. The OGSA has been designed to create, terminate, manage, and invoke stateful and transient grid services using standard interfaces and protocols. A transient service can be created and destroyed dynamically. Statefulness differentiates one service instance from another. Each service instance is identified by a globally unique grid service handle (GSH). Services are the building blocks of an OGSA-based grid. OGSA offers the following features in a heterogeneous, distributed grid environment:

- OGSA defines interfaces to facilitate service interoperability.
- OGSA delivers seamless QoS between the service components that include resources.
- OGSA manages resources.
- Delivers grid functionality using loosely coupled stateful services based on WSA.

The common services offered by the OGSA include (Fig. 1.16):

- **Infrastructure Services** are the services like naming, discovery required by other services.
- **Execution Management Services** are used to place, provision, and manage life cycle of various tasks, workflows, and services.

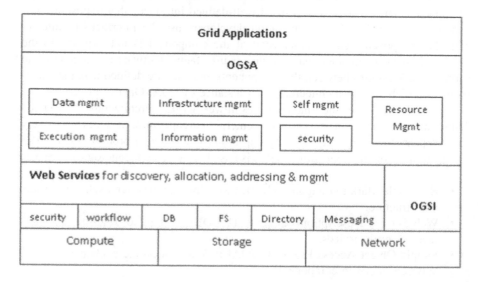

FIGURE 1.16   OGSA architecture.

- **Data Management Services** provide interfaces to represent, access, create and manage data. They handle data consistency, persistency, and data integrity issues.
- **Resource Management Services** provide interfaces to monitor, allocate, deploy and configure grid resources for a service.
- **Security Services** enforce security-related policies within a (virtual) organization. These services offer interfaces for authentication, authorization, and integrity assurance.
- **Information Services** provide interfaces to obtain information on the grid environment.
- **Self-Management Services** are autonomous services that help to attain QoS of a service.

Open grid service infrastructure (OGSI) provides formal and technical specifications of a grid service. Grid service interfaces correspond to port Types in WSDL. The set of port Types supported by a grid service form a service Type.

The third generation of grid further evolved using Semantic Web technologies to develop and deliver grid applications. Such a grid is called as a semantic grid. It uses:

- Autonomic computing to manage the heterogeneous grid resources. Its self-optimizing capability maximizes the utilization by tuning resources/jobs. It is able to anticipate failures and protects itself. This is called self-curing capability. It is able to diagnose failures and recover from them. Hence it possess self-healing capability. It is dynamic and capable of reconfiguring in case of changing environments. Hence it possess self-configuration capability.
- Business on Demand: The semantic grid is able to dynamically allocate resources based on the dynamic requirements of the virtual organization. For this resource, virtualization is a necessity.
- SOA offers loose coupling between grid services.
- Semantic services: Related services could be identified and grouped.

Some of the issues faced in grid computing include:

- A single job in a grid computing environment is voluminous. It is split into tasks that can be executed individually. The results are then gathered or orchestrated. As it is towards batch processing, it is not suitable for high-performance computing environments. Grid is highly suitable for high throughput computing applications where the entire job completion time is reduced rather than task completion time.
- Grid computing was promoted by scientific community. Hence lacked business benefits.
- Grid applications are platform-specific.
- It relies on volunteer computing to form a virtual organization when resources are free. This affects the availability and reliability of the resources to complete the grid job.

- Here the entire set of resources in a VO provides a single system image to the user. Many resources are virtualized as one. A job is split among many under-utilized resources. This might not be beneficial from the business point of view.

1.8 CLOUD COMPUTING

Cloud computing is a form of utility computing just like grid, where users pay for the computing resources used by them. Cloud [9] is defined as a parallel and distributed system consisting of a shared pool of abstracted, virtualized, dynamically managed computing resources (like storage, computing, platforms, network, applications) that are maintained in data centers. The resources are dynamically provisioned and reconfigured based on demand from the user. Hence resource management in cloud is elastic in nature. This is done automatically with less manual intervention. Hence services are abstracted from the user. SLA acts as a contract between the service provider and consumer. Users are then charged based on their usage of the computing resources. This forms a business model. From business point of view, this model reduces the capital and operational expenses of an organization.

1.8.1 CHARACTERISTICS OF CLOUD ENVIRONMENTS

Cloud computing models enable ubiquitous, convenient, on-demand network access to a shared pool of configurable computing resources. The following are the key characteristics of a cloud computing environment:

- Service-oriented architecture: All functionalities are offered to users as services through interfaces. These services can be easily extended, composed, orchestrated to offer the desired functionality to the user. SOA facilitates loose coupling and abstraction. Services can be customized to meet the user needs.
- *On-demand self-service*: Services can be provided dynamically, without human intervention as and when required by the user.
- *Broad network access*: The cloud provides services to heterogeneous client devices such as mobiles, laptops, and workstations through a standard network like the Internet.
- *Resource pooling*: The provider's resources are pooled and allocated/de-allocated to users dynamically, on-demand.
- *Rapid elasticity*: The resources in the cloud are dynamically provisioned and released on-demand as and when required by the application.
- *Measured service*: The services provided by the cloud can be metered and monitored.
- *Location independence*: Users access the cloud services anywhere and anytime through the Internet.
- Business Model: Cloud computing provides a business model for the IT

industry where the computing resource usage can be monitored. Payment can then be based on the usage of resources.

- Virtualization: This technology abstracts the hardware/software resources from the user. One physical resource is compartmentalized into many virtual resources that can be offered to various users. This has resulted in multi-tenancy where a single resource is utilized by many users. This in turn increases resource utilization and reduces the cost.

1.8.2 CLOUD MODELS

Cloud computing models are categorized based on their delivery of services or based on their deployment model. These two categories are discussed in the following section.

1.8.2.1 Cloud Services Models

The cloud services model defines the core functionality of the services implemented at different levels and delivered to the clients. Such delivery models (Fig. 1.17) can be categorized as follows:

- *Infrastructure as a Service* (*IaaS*) allows providers to set up and deliver virtualized hardware resources such as storage, compute, and networking to the users. Communication as a Service and Data storage as a Service are also some examples of IaaS. IaaS falls under the category of utility computing.
- *Platform as a Service* (*PaaS*) offers developers with the tools, platforms, and environment to build and deploy their applications on the cloud. It includes platforms for the development and deployment of services, environments for runtime execution, databases, APIs, etc. This is also termed as framework computing.

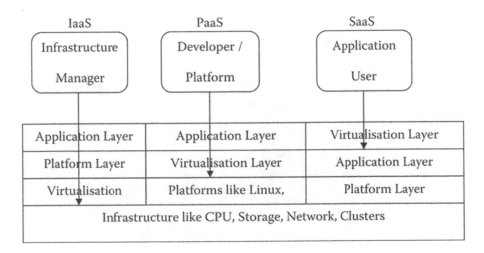

FIGURE 1.17 Cloud service models.

- *Software as a Service* (*SaaS*) offers applications operating in the cloud that can be accessed remotely on-demand as a service by the end-users. Users are thus freed from the burden of installing and using the required software locally. It is termed as business computing.

Following this, other services, such as database as a service and analytics as a service, can also be set up. Big Data as a Service (BDaaS) maintains and manages voluminous data on the cloud storage and offers continuous access of the same to its owner.

1.8.2.2   Cloud Deployment Models

Based on the functionality and accessibility of cloud services [9], the cloud offers four deployment models (Fig. 1.18):

- *Public cloud*: Users access the resources including infrastructure, frameworks, applications, and services provided by the service providers over the Internet. Users subscribe to the services they access and have to pay based on their usage.
- *Private cloud*: This type of cloud is in-premise and services are offered over the intranet. It is more secure when compared to a public cloud.
- *Hybrid cloud*: It is composed of multiple public/private clouds. This model offers the advantages of public and private deployment models.
- *Community cloud*: This can be a public/private cloud shared by a set of organizations under the same administrative domain.

NIST architecture of cloud is layered and is based on the essential characteristics of cloud at the top, followed by the delivery models and deployment models. The following are the advantages of the cloud model of distributed systems:

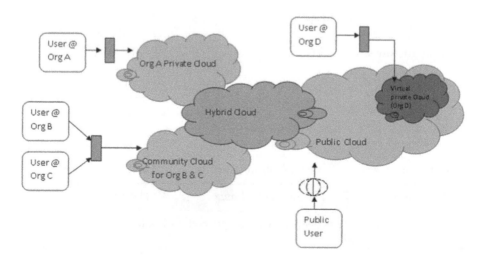

FIGURE 1.18   Cloud deployment models.

- Cost reduction: It reduces the Capital expenditure of purchase of equipment and operational expenditure of maintaining the cloud environment in an organization. Further, the operational expenditure including power, wages, and upgradation is shared by all the users.
- Better flexibility and scalability as new infrastructures can be added on the fly without affecting the services being offered.
- Better resource utilization as the same resource is shared virtually among many users.
- Data backup and disaster recovery are handled automatically by the service providers.
- Cloud resources can be used anywhere anytime using any access technology by the users.
- Cloud resources are highly available as another instance can be started on failure of the existing instance.

Some of the challenges faced in cloud computing include:

- Reliable Internet Connection should be available to access the resources.
- Security of customer's data is managed by the service providers.
- Dependency on cloud service providers/vendors.

1.9   OTHER COMPUTING PARADIGMS

1.9.1   Ubiquitous Computing

This section compares ubiquitous, pervasive, and mobile computing. Desktop computing enables a user to carry out computing functionalities using a single desktop. Here a single desktop is used by a single user. Ubiquitous computing moves to the era when invisible resources are used by many users. It is a many-many relationship. Ubiquitous computing, which means "omnipresent". Cloud is a ubiquitous environment as users can access the remote resources hosted in the cloud using Internet and various access technologies. Even though resources do not move, these resources can be accessed from any location using Internet. Hence mobility is high. A pervasive computing environment embeds computing in various devices like IoT. The resources are much smaller when compared to that of mobile systems. Mobility of such systems is low. They are used in applications like smart homes. Mobile computing embeds computing in devices carried by the user. Mobile computing involves mobile communication, mobile hardware, and mobile software. The mobility of such systems is high. Computing using cell phones comes under this category. The main characteristics of ubiquitous computing are:

- seamless access to remote information resources and fault-tolerant communication
- when compared to pervasive and mobile computing, the user does not possess the resources and hence does not have control over the remote resources.
- The user can access the resource anytime, anywhere using suitable access and communication technologies.

The major limitations of ubiquitous computing include:

- Limitations of network bandwidth and network coverage.
- Battery-powered devices are energy-constrained.
- Security risks on using various access devices and public networks.
- Size of Input/output screens of mobile and pervasive devices.

1.9.2 Jungle Computing

Traditional high-performance computing was restricted to supercomputers. The emerge of clusters, grid, and cloud computing paradigms also facilitated high-performance computing as the tasks could be executed in parallel in various worker nodes. Various high-performance computing infrastructures like supercomputing, grid, and cloud can be connected using a huge high-speed communication network. Such an ensemble of heterogeneous systems forms a "Computing Jungle" (Fig. 1.19) When a user submits an application, the middleware identifies which HiPC infrastructure is best. It then uses suitable tools to compile and deploy the application in the infrastructure. Communication network ensures communication between various HiPC infrastructures and the user.

Task complexity decides the computing environment. Hence a suitable high-performance computing environment may be chosen based on the task's needs. Some of the characteristics of jungle computing include:

- Resource independence and heterogeneity: Resources differed considerably in their storage and processing capabilities. Hence a middleware is needed to hide details of the resources from the user.

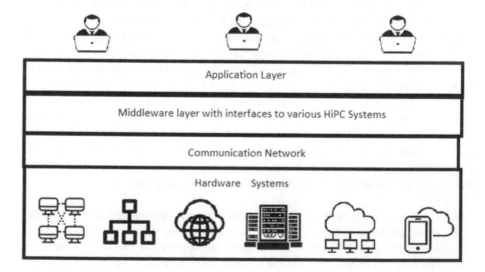

FIGURE 1.19 Jungle computing.

- Middleware: Each HiPC system has its own middleware. The Compute Jungle's middleware ensures interoperability between them.
- Robust connectivity ensures reliable communication with HiPC systems in the jungle.
- Unique resource identification overcomes resource conflicts.
- Malleability provides flexibility to adapt to changes in the resources.
- Fault-tolerance to handle system failures and restore application state.
- Automated conversion from serial to parallel code. This feature eliminates the need for expertise in parallel programming paradigm.
- Middleware also integrates legacy codes with Jungle software.

The major limitations of jungle computing include:

- Management of resources belonging to different administrative domains.
- Difficulty in interconnecting various high-performance computing systems.
- When a particular computing environment is chosen on the fly, system software like compilers and executable application code created face interoperability issues.

1.9.3   FOG COMPUTING

The major issue in cloud computing is that all the data has to be transferred to Centralized Computer Clusters to carry out the computations. This involves network latency. We all might know about Hadoop framework used for processing big data in a cloud environment. The basic concept of Hadoop is to move compute close to data located in a particular data node. By doing so data movement is minimized and network latency is reduced. A similar situation also occurs in fog computing. Here processing and storage resources are typically located near the network edge, close to the devices generating information. So fog computing is more suitable for latency-aware applications like smart city, healthcare, and augmented reality. Fog computing is a virtualized platform, where computing resources like processor, storage, and network are placed at the edge of the cloud, instead of establishing communication channels for cloud storage and processing. Typically the processing is done between the user and the cloud. Cloud can be used to process applications that are not real-time and for long-term storage of data.

Some of the characteristics of fog computing [10] are

- Proximity of frequently used data and computing to end-users.
- Location-aware processing reduces latency.
- Geographically distributed processing ensures scalability and speed.
- Promotes usage of sensor networks to gather data.
- Supports location-based mobility.
- Promotes real-time data processing at the edge of the network.
- Supports heterogeneous resources and interoperability between them.
- Can be optimized according to users as the fog server is directed networked to the user.

- Fog localization and cloud globalization facilitate better analytics by filtering the data at the edge and performing globalized analysis or localized analysis.

Some of the other paradigms highly related to fog computing are (Fig. 1.20):

- Mobile cloud computing (MCC): Mobile devices are resource-constrained and hence may not be able to execute some services. Hence a lightweight cloud server called cloudlet is used at the network edge to overcome the resource constraints of mobile devices. The main constraint is reliable low-latency networking to edge servers.
- Mobile edge computing (MEC): A mobile edge computing (MEC) server is collocated at the base stations of cellular networks. MEC server provides computing and storage facilities. A user request is forwarded to MEC for processing. If MEC cannot process the request, it is forwarded to the cloud server.

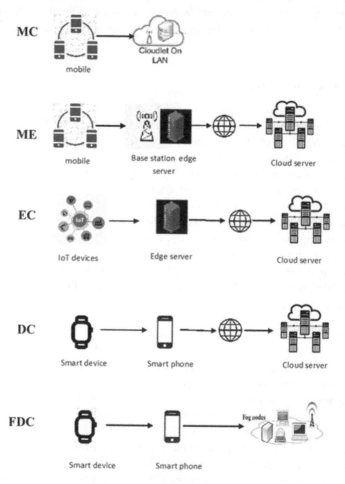

FIGURE 1.20   Paradigms related to fog computing.

- Edge computing (EC): In an IoT environment, it is preferred to carry out computation closer to the data sources (sensors). Hence such processors not only consume data from sensors but also produce data by processing them. Edge device is located between the data source and the cloud server. Cloudlet servers as an edge of the mobile app and cloud whereas an IoT gateway serves as an edge between IoT sensors and cloud. A smartphone serves as an edge for the application and cloud. They can perform computing, cache data, or store data. Edge servers can also offload data or get services from the cloud. Edge servers can also service clients on behalf of cloud servers. While edge computing is based on devices, fog is based on processors located in the LAN. Edge and Fog computing aim to move computing closer to the device and decentralize it.
- Dew computing (DC): aims to realize the potential of on-premise computers/ smartphones in collaboration with cloud services. It aims to use the full potential of local and cloud systems. It is based on micro server-based architecture. Although Fog servers are connected to cloud, it need not use the cloud services. In dew computing, data from fit bit-like devices is transferred through smartphones to the cloud and processed. Hence cloud services are always used in dew computing.
- Fog-Dew Computing (FDC): IoT devices are connected to the fog server through local connections. Fog server is connected to cloud through Internet connections. So it can compute offline in fog servers or online in cloud servers.

Architecture of a fog computing system at a high level consists of three layers [11–13] (Fig. 1.21):

- Bottom most layer consists of IoT plate plane. This layer consists of all connected devices that perform sensing and actuation functionalities.
- Fog layer: uses virtual and physical resources. This layer can perform small and medium-level data processing. Usually for time-sensitive applications, processing is done in this layer. It accumulates sensor data, processes it, and sends actuation signals to the IoT plane. Virtualization of resources is also possible. Usually, container virtualization is done in this layer. This layer can also obtain services from the cloud layer.
- Cloud layer: This layer performs complex data processing and storage. If the application is not time-sensitive, then fog layer obtains services from application layer to process the application.

The users can obtain services from the fog layer or the cloud layer.

1.9.4 OSMOTIC COMPUTING

Cloud environment provides the required resources (including computing and storage) to carry out the functionality of conventional IoT applications. Such a centralized framework introduces unnecessary delay for latency-sensitive

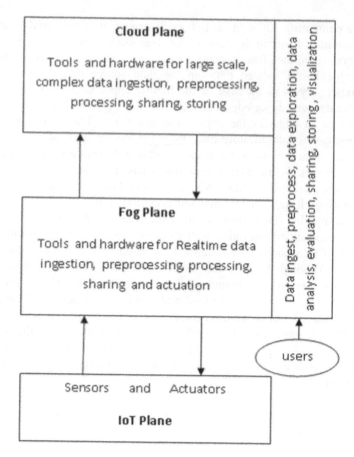

FIGURE 1.21 Architecture of fog computing system.

IoT applications. Latency-aware applications need to be processed at the edge of the network close to the devices where data is generated/used. Hence depending on the nature of the applications, cloud and edge models need to coexist and co-operate. The need for a seamless integration of the cloud-edge platforms can be successful only with supportive services for interoperability, privacy, and management. Osmotic computing facilitates cooperative usage of such services in edge-cloud environment. For this lightweight virtualization mechanisms are suitable. Hence, osmotic computing uses containerization and microservices extensively.

A software application is composed up of a number of independently deployable modular microservices. Each microservice executes a unique process and communicates through a well-defined, lightweight mechanism, such as a container. A container encapsulates software components and ensures reduced deployment overhead. Thus container-based approach facilitates deployment of lightweight microservices at the devices in the network edge.

Osmotic computing thus facilitates efficient execution of IoT microservices between cloud datacenter and the network edge by providing increased resource and data management capabilities at the edge of the network. It also supports suitable data transfer protocols for seamless integration of services. Osmotic computing provides automatic and secure microservice deployment in heterogeneous cloud-edge environment by using lightweight containers like dockers. It aims at highly distributed and federated environments, and enables the automatic deployment of microservices that are composed and interconnected over both edge and cloud infrastructures.

Osmotic computing facilitates service migration across cloud, fog, and edge computing resources [14]. It is derived from the term "osmosis" which refers to the equalization of the concentration of a solution by allowing the molecules of the solvent to move from a region of lower solute concentration to a higher solute concentration through a semi-permeable membrane. The chemical solution is analogous to the computational infrastructure of the fog environment whose resource requirements change based on the application and time. Osmotic computing aims to balance the load by utilizing the resources suitably in cloud, fog, and device layers. This load balancing is achieved by migrating the services across the cloud, fog, and device layers.

The major elements of the osmosis process include solute, solvent, solution, semi-permeable membrane, concentration. An analogy can be drawn from these components to osmotic computing as follows:

- *Solute*: These particles are not allowed to migrate. We can draw an analogy to solute in the computing infrastructure as computational power, storage, energy, etc. depending on the application.
- *Solvent*: The solvent can migrate between the solutions through a semi-permeable membrane. An analogy to the same in computing infrastructure is services. These services can migrate between the cloud, fog, and edge infrastructure to improve the effectiveness of the application.
- *Solution*: Comprises solute and solvent. An analogy to the solution includes the complete infrastructure comprising of the users, devices, computing/ storage resources, platforms, and services.
- *Semi-permeable membrane*: controls the movement of the solvent to equalize the concentration of the solutions. The fog computing environment performs this functionality in the osmotic computing framework by deciding on when, where, and how the microservices are to be migrated. The resource allocators decide when the microservices should migrate between the cloud, fog, and edge resources based on the application. Based on the resource availability, latency, and load balancing factors, microservice can be migrated from one resource to another. The technology support for migration may include lightweight container services.
- *Concentration*: This represents the ratio of the microservices to be handled by the resources available at various layers including device, fog, and cloud.

Osmotic computing model is thus based on the osmosis principle. The user plane interacts with the fog layer resource managers which classify the services into micro and macro services based on the application needs. These resource managers act as a semi-permeable membrane to migrate services between edge resources and cloud resources to improve the application performance.

Here the application is modeled as a directed graph with data transformation tasks as its nodes, and dataflow between these tasks as edges. This graph model allows the distribution and execution of the tasks across the resources available in the cloud, edge, and device layers. These data transformation tasks are also called as microelements (MEL) that encapsulate resources, services, and data. An MEL encapsulates one of the following categories (Fig. 1.22) [15]:

- Microservices (MS), which offer particular functionality and can be easily deployed or migrated,
- Microdata (MD), which represent information flow to and from a sensor or actuator or data centers,
- Microcomputing (MC), which executes different types of computational tasks (e.g., statistical analysis, error checking, or machine learning) using a mixture of real-time and historic MD data, or
- Microactuator (MA), which controls the state of a physical resource at the network edge.

IoT applications are decomposed into a number of interacting atomic MELs that perform a simple functionality like gathering data from a sensor, performing a simple transformation of data, etc. These MELs are deployed in containers like dockers that are hosted in edge or cloud resources. MELs. MELs may be deployed and orchestrated across both cloud and edge resources. MELs encapsulate simple functionalities in a lightweight virtual environment like container. This enables dynamic deployment and migration of MELs across heterogeneous systems. Hosting MELs in containers enables

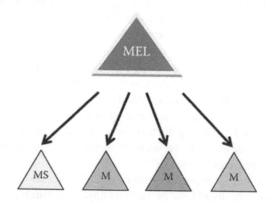

FIGURE 1.22   Categorization of MEL.

- Isolation among *MELs* belonging to different applications.
- Execution of MELs on heterogeneous infrastructures like edge, cloud, and device based on the application.
- MEL graph composition and orchestration based on the application.

This enhances the scalability and dynamism of IoT applications.

Consider a use case of a fire detection and alarm system using drones. Some of the activities include capturing videos by cameras in drones, color extraction, object detection, transferring identified frames to cloud, and analyzing frames from multiple drones, activity detection, report generation, and alarm generation. Microservices can be created for these activities. It includes processing (video analytics) and data management functionality. The application is initiated with video capture by the drones. The resource managers in the fog layer decide on where and when the various microservices are to be executed. These microservices can be executed in the device, edge, or cloud layers. This decision is based on factors like latency in data transfer, resource availability, and the application characteristics. The entire application can be modeled as a directed graph with nodes representing the data transformation tasks and the edges representing the dataflow dependencies between the transformation tasks.

The activities in the fire detection and alarm case study can be decomposed into a number of MELs that can be orchestrated as shown in Fig. 1.23:

- Video capturing using cameras in drones as a MEL in device layer (MEL1).
- Color extraction using simple computational algorithms as a MEL in the device layer (MEL2).
- Transferring frames to edge data centers as a MEL in the device layer (MEL3).
- Object detection as a MEL in the edge layer (MEL4).
- Transferring identified frames to cloud as a MEL in the edge layer (MEL5).
- Analyzing frames from multiple drones as a MEL in the cloud layer (MEL6).
- Activity detection as a MEL in the cloud layer (MEL7).
- Report generation as a MEL in the cloud layer (MEL8).
- Notification generation as a MEL in the cloud layer (MEL9).
- Transfer of notification to actuators in the device layer as a MEL in the cloud layer (MEL10).
- Alarm generation by actuating the alarm in the device layer as a MEL in the device layer (MEL11).

Osmotic computing deals with dynamic migration of microservices between cloud and edge data centers to ensure reliable and quality IoT-related services including latency, reliability, networking, load balancing, availability security, privacy. The microservices are thus provisioned in a federated edge–cloud environment. The bidirectional flow of adapted microservices from cloud to edge must be managed. Decoupling of network management from data is facilitated using software-defined networking. IoTSim-Osmosis is a simulator for osmotic computing environment. It can simulate and run osmotic applications between edge and cloud resources.

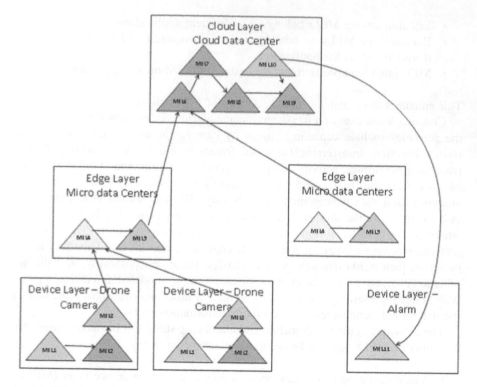

FIGURE 1.23   MEL graph for the case study.

Network is simulated with dynamic SDN and SD-WAN. It provides facilities to simulate dynamic routing mechanisms and multilevel optimization mechanisms.

1.10   RESEARCH DIRECTIONS

To ensure seamless integration of services at cloud, fog, and device layers in the distributed environment, active research is being done in the following areas [16]:

Microservice configuration: In conventional architecture suitable cloud resources are selected to configure virtual machines (VMs) based on quality of service (QoS) constraints. In osmotic computing, micro services are preferred when compared to heavy weight VMs. In such a federated cloud-edge environment, it is necessary to automate configuration of microservices in both cloud and edge datacenters. Suitable multi-criteria optimization and decision making techniques have to utilize to automatically configure these microservices.

Microservice networking: In traditional cloud based IoT systems, data is transferred to the cloud that hosts services to manipulate and process the application data. In such an environment, the services do not migrate. In osmotic computing based on the needs of the applications, micro services can be migrated to/from the cloud/edge resources. The microservices behavior changes according to the *application*/user requirements. So flexible and configurable networking is required. Software-defined networking (SDN) and network function virtualization (NFV) support in-network data processing (between edge and datacenter). It also provides network management abstraction by separating data and management layers of the network. Federated networks can be used to manage the heterogeneous cloud-edge environment.

- *Microservice security*: An osmotic computing framework needs a coherent and consistent security policy within both the cloud datacenter and the edge computing environments to enable microservice execution and migration. Ensuring that the same security considerations are observed for a particular micro service across both environments remains a challenge. This necessitates self-identification of services in the federated edge – cloud environment and building suitable trust mechanisms.
- *Reverse offloading*: Traditional systems offload computing in IoT devices to the cloud. Osmotic computing also offers reverse offloading that aims at offloading computation done in a cloud resource to an edge device. Hence it is essential to identify suitable microservices that can be executed in the edge devices when compared to cloud environment to reduce latency and improve the performance of the application.
- *Micro service workload contention*: In a federated osmotic environment, co-deployment of related microservices is essential. But co-deployed containerized microservices leads to workload contention. Thus understanding the nature of their composition is critical to deciding which microservices can be deployed together. Container engines like Docker Swarm, and Kubernetes should be studied to handle such resource contentions dynamically among co-deployed microservices across cloud and edge datacenter resources by analyzing the performance, prioritizing workload, and coordinating their deployment
- *Resource monitoring*: Traditional tools monitor CPU, memory, file system, and network usage statistics but not microservice-level violations in QoS metrics. Hence scalable methods to monitor QoS and security metrics across multiple levels of micro services in cloud and edge data centers.
- *Microservice orchestration and composition*: A suitable technique to predict workload and performance of co-located microservices across cloud-edge datacenters along with QoS aware resource orchestration and composition technique is essential. This enables effective offloading and reverse offloading of microservices of the application between edge and cloud resources.
- *Scheduling*: Scheduling of suitable resources in cloud and grid environments is an important area of research. Various factors like job size, latency, utilization, energy saving have to be considered. Statistical and evolutionary optimization techniques have been tried.

1.11 CONCLUSION

This chapter provided an overview of various computing paradigms starting from parallel processing systems to distributed systems. In the centralized computing paradigm, all the computer resources, such as processors, memory, and storage are located in one physical system and controlled centrally. Resources are shared among various processes under one operating system. While such systems can offer high security, integrity, low maintenance, and reliability, they suffer from scalability and inflexibility. A parallel computing paradigm enables the execution of computations in parallel. Typically, processors share a central memory and communicate through the shared memory in a tightly coupled manner. Alternatively, they can be loosely coupled having distributed memory. Communication in this case is through message passing. Cluster computing paradigm uses a cluster of computers. It is a type of parallel or distributed processing system, consisting of a collection of interconnected standalone computers that work cooperatively as a single, integrated computing resource. The main characteristic of this model is centralized control. Distributed computing (Fig. 1.24) consists of a collection of independent computers, each having its own memory, disk, and processor. These independent nodes work cooperatively with each other to solve a problem. The participating computers communicate with each other through message passing and the group appears to be a single coherent system to its users. When a distributed system possesses decentralized control, it becomes a P2P system. A grid is a distributed system with the concept of virtual organization where a number of physical resources are aggregated to perform a task cooperatively. Cloud computing is a distributed Internet-based computing environment. In cloud, shared resources can be provisioned on-demand. Clouds facilitate the offering of computing services as a utility analogous to electricity or water supply. The advent of the Internet fostered Web hosting, even prior to cloud computing. Web hosting is the mechanism of providing space in the WWW to host one server. For example, application service providers can host their applications on WWW servers to deliver applications as services to their customers. This approach limits the number of users of the service provided. Using virtualization, this model could be made more effective and financially viable. This gave rise to the concept of offering SaaS to a larger number of users. Eventually, SaaS grew in popularity due to the ease of use,

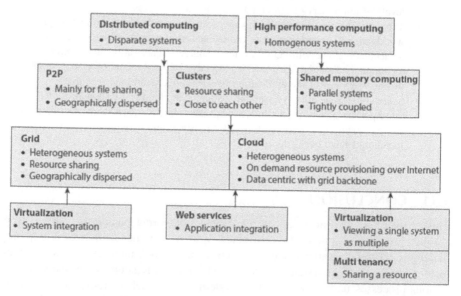

FIGURE 1.24 Distributed computing paradigms.

giving rise to what is today known as cloud, where not only software but also platform (PaaS) and infrastructure (IaaS) could be offered as a service. In the current cloud technology, however, it is possible to provide anything and everything as a service, which gave rise to the term anything-as-a-service (XaaS). Analytics could also be offered as a service. While cloud computing was motivated by the business community, grid computing was motivated by the scientific community. Later cloud computing was enhanced to fog computing to provide services for IoT devices. Other fog computing-related paradigms include mobile cloud computing, mobile edge computing, dew computing, fog dew computing, and edge computing. Osmotic computing has enabled seamless migration of microservices among the various layers of the fog computing environment. The next chapter will provide a discussion on edge computing systems.

REFERENCES

1. Pete Sanderson. (2019, August 7).Top 10 reasons to major in Computer Science. https://www.collegexpress.com/interests/science-and-engineering/articles/careers-science-engineering/top-10-reasons-major-computer-science/.
3. Hwang, K., Fox, G. C., & Dongarra, J. J. (2012). *Distributed and cloud computing: From parallel processing to the Internet of things.* Morgan Kaufmann, United States.
2. Gill, S. (2015, April). Impacts of computers on today's society. *International Journal of Core Engineering & Management (IJCEM)*, 2(1), 173–178.
4. Barkallah, H. (2017). Evolution of the distributed computing paradigms: A brief road map. *International Journal of Computing*, 6, 233–249.
5. Kshemkalyani, A. D., & Singhal, M. (2011, March 1). *Distributed computing: Principles, algorithms, and systems*(1st ed.). Cambridge University Press, New York, United States of America.
6. Tanenbum, A. S., & Van Steen, M. (2015). *Distributed systems: Principles and paradigms.* Pearson, United States.
7. Couloris, G., Dollimore, J., Kindberg, T., & Blair, G. (2012). *Distributed systems: Concepts and design*(5th ed.). Pearson, United States of America.
8. Abbas, A. (2016). *Grid computing: A practical guide to technology and applications* (1st ed.). Laxmi Publications, New Delhi, India.
9. Buyya, R., Yeo, C. S., Venugopal, S., Broberg, J., & Brandic, I. (2009). Cloud computing and emerging IT platforms: Vision, hype, and reality for delivering computing as the 5th utility. *Future Generation Computer Systems*, 25(6), 599–616.
10. Naha, R. K., Garg, S., & Chan, A. Fog-computing architecture: Survey and challenges (Computing, 2019), Big Data-Enabled Internet of Things, Chap. 10, pp. 199–223. DOI: 10.1049/PBPC025E_ch10, IET Digital Library. https://digital-library.theiet.org/content/ books /10.1049/pbpc025e_ch10.
11. Buyya, R., & Srirama, S. N. (2019, January 30). *Fog and edge computing: Principles and paradigms*1st ed.). Wiley, United States.
12. Al-Qamash, A., Soliman, I., Abulibdeh, R., & Saleh, M. (2018). Cloud, fog, and edge computing: A Software Engineering perspective. In *2018 International Conference on Computer and Applications (ICCA)*. Beirut, 276–284. doi: 10.1109/COMAPP.201 8.8460443.
13. Naha, R. N., S., Garg, Georgakopoulos, D., Jayaraman, P. P., Gao, L., Xian, Y., & Ranjan, R. (2018). Fog computing: Survey of trends, architectures, requirements, and research directions. *IEEE Access, 6*, 47980–48009. doi: 10.1109/ACCESS.2018. 2866491.

14. Sharma, V., Srinivasan, K., Jayakody, D., Rana, O., & Kumar, R. (2017). Managing service-heterogeneity using osmotic computing. ArXiv abs/1704.04213.
15. Villari, M., Fazio, M., Dustdar, S., Rana, O., Jha, D. N., & Ranjan, R. (2019, August). Osmosis: The osmotic computing platform for microelements in the cloud, edge, and Internet of Things. *Computer*, *52*(8), 14–26. doi: 10.1109/MC.2018.2888767.
16. Villari, M., Fazio, M., Dustdar, S., Rana, O., & Ranjan, R. (2016). Osmotic computing: A new paradigm for edge/cloud integration. *IEEE Cloud Computing*, *3*(6), 76–83. doi: 10.1109/MCC.2016.124.

2 Edge Computing and Its Essentials

2.1 INTRODUCTION

Consider a smart building with video cameras to detect the movement of people. Video signal is continuously streamed to the cloud server. The motion detection application in the cloud server can detect features and store to the database. As large volume of video data is streamed continuously to the cloud, significant network bandwidth is consumed. The cloud server should also analyze the video footage from all the cameras simultaneously. These issues can be overcome if the motion detection application could be executed close to the cameras. Only the required clips can then be transferred to the cloud for further analysis and storage.

Traditionally, real-time data collected from various sensors is propagated uplink to cloud servers for further processing and storage. The cloud infrastructure is highly suitable to process such large amount of continuously changing heterogeneous data also termed as big data. But, big data processing in distant cloud infrastructure fails when data sources are distributed across multiple locations and processing is to be done near real-time. This motivates the need for an alternative paradigm that is capable of performing computations closer to the sensors or data sources. Such an infrastructure located at the edge of the network is capable of performing low latency computations, aggregating the data, and then transferring it to the cloud for further analysis. Also, downstream responses from the cloud are returned to these nodes. The edge of the network can be a room, a building, or a campus based on the network coverage.

It becomes essential to process voluminous data generated by IoT devices in real-time in proximity to data sources using edge computing infrastructure. This not only reduces latency in computation and usage of networking resources but also enforces data security. This section discusses the evolution of edge computing paradigm through the technology preparation phase, rapid growth phase, and stabilization phase [1].

Technology preparation phase started off with content development networks (CDN). CDNs with geographically distributed caching servers enabled users to access the nearest server (1998). Network traffic and latency were decreased. While CDN emphasizes on data caching, edge computing focuses on function caching. In 2005, function caching was applied for personalized mailbox management to reduce latency. Cloudlet (2009) was used to downstream cloud information to network edge. Edge data processing initially started with mobile devices (2010). Mobile edge computing (MEC) emphasizes the establishment of edge servers between the cloud server and edge devices for offloading computations. The concept of fog computing was fostered by CISCO (2012). Fog computing focuses on a virtualized

DOI: 10.1201/9781003230946-2

computing platform to migrate cloud tasks to the network edge. While fog computing aims at optimizing communication at the infrastructure level, edge computing (2013) focuses on computing and network resources at the device, edge server, and cloud server layers. Cloud-sea computing emphasizes on the cloud end and human/physical world end of the system. But, edge computing concentrates on the communication path (upstream and downstream) between the cloud and the IoT devices.

Since 2015 edge computing has attracted more attention from industry and academia. In 2015 edge computing gained its formal definition from "Edge computing: Vision and challenges" white paper. The paper defined edge computing as an enabling technology allowing computation to be performed at the edge of the network, on downstream data on behalf of cloud services, and on upstream data on behalf of IoT services. In 2016 NSF in collaboration with Intel established information center networks in wireless edge networks (ICN-WEN). NSF Workshop on Grand Challenges (2016) and edge computing symposium in China (2017) exposed the technology to the scientific community. LinuxEdgeX – the common open framework for IoT edge computing was built in 2017. The year 2018 saw active industrial participation in development of edge computing platforms. Automotive Edge Computing Consortium was formed in 2018. The first book on edge computing was also published in this year. Kubernetes used in both cloud and device environments was developed collaboratively by Cloud Native Computing Foundation (CNCF) and Eclipse Foundation in 2019. The usage of edge computing in healthcare domain was focused in the Bio-World Conference and Expos (2019). This rapid growth trend is expected to stabilize in 2021.

Edge computing analyses data by harnessing the compute power of the resources outside of traditional data centers. These computational resources are located in proximity to the data sources. Data caching/storage, data processing, service delivery, IoT management, and privacy protection are some of the services offered by this layer. Edge computing environment up-streams data from devices to cloud servers and down-streams data from cloud servers to the devices.

When cloud computing was introduced, all the computations were shifted to the cloud. Due to network latency and the transmission cost, it is more logical to perform related tasks at the network edge. With the improvement of the processing power and capability, the amount of tasks performed on the edge will continue to grow [2]. The major advantages of edge computing include:

- Reduction in computation latency to meet the customer demands.
- Reduction in network bandwidth.
- Preservation of data security and privacy.
- Good reliability even on network failures.
- Reduction in operational costs due to communication, storage, and processing.
- Better data governance due to improvement in quality and usability of data.
- Improved scalability of cloud by computation offloading to the network edge.

The major components of an edge computing system [3] (Fig. 2.1) include:

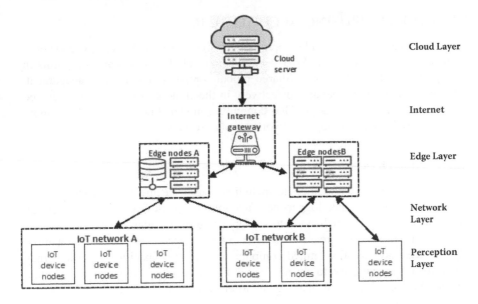

FIGURE 2.1 High-level architecture of an edge computing system.

Perception layer: It consists of the edge devices. An edge device is a special-purpose cost-effective hardware designed to perform a specific task effectively. The edge device has limited compute/storage resources. Some examples of such devices include transducers, sensors, actuators, logs, and cameras that perform functionality of gathering and/or transmitting data. Some edge devices have processing power to do additional activities. Analytics applications on image, video, text data gathered by these devices need to be deployed and managed based on the resource availability [4].

Networking layer: It is responsible for connecting devices, edge systems, and cloud systems. It comprises various communication and data transfer protocols.

Edge computing layer: The major components in this layer include the edge server and gateways. An edge server has higher computational/storage capacity when compared to an IoT device. Workload that cannot be carried out in a resource-constrained edge device can be done using these general-purpose compute nodes or a cluster of nodes. Edge gateways in this layer perform specialized network functions including protocol mapping, network termination, and tunneling and firewall protection.

Application or processing layer: This layer is responsible to carry out complex data-intensive tasks and to store voluminous data. Private or public cloud servers in this layer act as repositories for sharing data among the nodes. Cloud servers perform complex data-intensive/compute-intensive applications that cannot be hosted in edge servers. Cloud servers can also be used for resource allocation and job management at the edge nodes.

Apart from the above-mentioned components, a suitable interface is to be provided for the users to monitor, manage, and interact with the system. The next section will provide a detailed architecture of the edge computing system.

2.2 EDGE COMPUTING ARCHITECTURE

By considering edge and cloud computing paradigms as complementary, a synergy can be reached between them. Edge servers can handle latency-aware computing in close proximity to data sources. Shared global computation/storage, management, and data privacy can be handled effectively in the cloud server. Fig. 2.1 discussed the various layers of a generic edge computing model. Fig. 2.2 provides a more detailed view [5] considering a network of edge servers.

2.2.1 EDGE DEVICES

Devices that collect data in the site including sensors, cameras, microphones, recorders, web monitors, data loggers can function as edge devices. Edge devices can also be actuators and visualization tools. Objective of the edge device is to collect information and send upstream or transfer information downstream for actuation. Edge devices have usually limited compute and storage capacity. Sometimes they can have higher capacity to do additional functionalities. Edge devices contain transducers that convert physical signals to electrical and vice-versa.

2.2.2 EDGE SERVER CLUSTER

When a distributed peer-to-peer connection of edge servers is considered, some edge servers may be close to a particular edge device while others may be far away. Computation and storage are replicated in multiple edge server nodes. The edge servers can be present at the device edge or at the network edge. Some workloads can be processed at the device edge maintained close to the sensor/actuator. Other workloads have to be migrated across to other edge servers called as local edge servers, where they can be processed. These servers may be farther away from the device but within the network edge. Workloads include both application workload (that includes compute and storage) and network tasks. As the local edge contains more resources they can perform complex computing and networking functionalities.

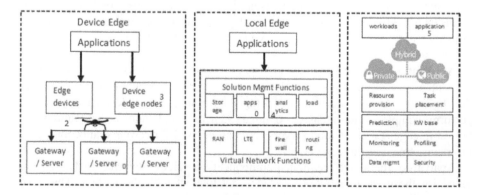

FIGURE 2.2 Edge computing – a detailed architecture.

Device edge nodes only perform simple functionalities. The compute nodes perform less compute-intensive operations. The gateway nodes additionally perform simple networking functions from the device to the local edge. Network latency involved may be in microseconds. Communication protocols between the devices and between the device and the local edge work over shorter distances and consume low power. Edge devices with additional functionalities act as device edge nodes.

Local edge nodes have additional compute, storage, and network capability. Such edge nodes can be used for computation. A small-scale data center (cluster of nodes) at the network edge called the cloudlet can be used. Such a cloudlet can store data at the network edge, host intelligent applications (like video/text analytics) to process data, and filter data to be transferred upstream to the cloud. Network latency may be in tens to hundreds of milliseconds.

Network function virtualization handles networking functions (like load balancing, security) with software-based technologies (called virtual network functions (VNFs)) rather than hardware. VNFs decouple software from the underlying hardware. This offers flexibility to vendors to create a more scalable and agile network using software functions. Some of the networking functionalities provided by VNF at the local edge include routing, firewall, Radio Access Network (RAN), Evolved Packet Core (EPC) framework for a 4G Long-Term Evolution (LTE) network. Protocols used between the edge server and the cloud have large throughput and high speed. Data caching and filtering, visualization, real-time computation, and control are common tasks done at the edge level. Resource allocation and management is a major issue. Usually, cloud servers handle it.

2.2.3 Cloud Server

The server is used to perform complex computation, resource allocation and management, data summarization, and secure data storage. Resource management defined by software framework in the cloud offers middleware services to manage the resources of the entire system and maintains quality of service for the applications. These services aim to balance application latency and cost by choosing a suitable resource for a task either in the device, edge server, or cloud server layer. Some of the services offered in this layer include:

- Data management service is used to access information stored in various SQL and NoSQL data stores.
- Monitoring service keeps track of the current status of applications and resources in the entire system (edge and cloud).
- Knowledge base maintains past information on resource/application demands.
- Profiler creates resource/application profiles based on historical information in the knowledge base and as well as current information obtained from the monitoring services.
- Performance prediction service forecasts the resource utilization and performance based on the historical information on resource demands. This in turn affects the application performance.

- Resource provisioning service allocates both cloud and edge resources dynamically for various tasks based on the information provided by the monitoring, profiling, prediction services, and user requirements.
- Task placement service aims at identifying a suitable resource at the device, edge, or cloud layer to execute the task effectively. It uses the information from the resource provisioning service.
- Security service provides the required authentication, authorization, and confidentiality for various applications.

Consider a use case of a fire detection system using drones. Activities done in different layers of the system include:

- Video analytics software to detect fire and network functionality for the application is deployed in the device edge and local edge.
- Drones capture videos. Initial video processing (like color extraction) may be done in the drones and device edge.
- Captured frames are sent to local edge for object detection (a more complex functionality).
- Frames after object detection are transferred to cloud for further management. In cloud, data from multiple drones may be analyzed to detect an activity and report.
- If retraining is required in device or local edge, a new model may be trained in the cloud and uploaded in the network edge.

The following sections discuss devices and networking protocols commonly used for edge computing.

2.3   BACKGROUND ESSENTIALS: IOT DEVICES

Smart objects in Internet of Things system need to be context-aware and interact with the environment. So, environmental attributes are obtained by these smart objects through sensors. They also cause actions to the surrounding environment using actuators. Transducers convert signals from one form to another. Sensors and actuators are transducers. IoT sensors are mostly small in size, cost-effective, and consume less power. They are energy-constrained. Some of the common sensors are listed:

2.3.1   Mobile Phone-Based Sensors

Smartphones have inbuilt sensors and data processing capabilities. Smartphones can be used to sense various physical elements.

- Movement patterns like walking and running can be sensed using accelerometers. Mechanical, capacitive, and piezoelectric accelerometers are common.
- Orientation can be sensed using gyroscope.
- Visual and audio information can be collected using camera and microphone.

- Magnetic fields detected using magnetometer can be used to find direction and presence of metals.
- Location of the phone can be detected using global positioning system (GPS)
- Intensity of the ambient light can be sensed using light sensor.
- Distance/proximity can be measured using the proximity sensors that use an infrared (IR) LED, which emits IR rays.

Sensors to measure temperature, atmospheric pressure, and humidity like thermometers, barometers, and humidity sensors may also be available in smartphones. Some of the applications that use sensor data and computing capabilities of smartphones include:

- Activity detection using camera, microphone, accelerometer sensors from smartphones.
- Fitness applications that use sensors in smartphones to track physical activities, diet, exercises, and lifestyle.
- Analyzing smoking pattern and mental health can also be done using sensors and computing capabilities of smartphones.

2.3.2 MEDICAL SENSORS

Wearable devices can remotely monitor the health of a patient using medical sensors to measure the heart rate, pulse, blood pressure, body temperature, respiration rate, and blood glucose level. Wearable devices in the form of smartwatches, wristbands, monitoring patches, and smart textiles can be used to monitor the vital health parameters of the patient. Data measured from these sensors should be related to the contextual information to draw correct inference.

2.3.3 NEURAL SENSORS

These sensors use electroencephalography (EEG) to read various brainwaves including alpha, beta, gamma, theta, and delta waves. Based on this the brain activity can be deduced to manage stress, for improved learning and mental health.

2.3.4 ENVIRONMENTAL AND CHEMICAL SENSORS

These sensors are used to obtain environmental parameters like temperature, humidity, pressure, water pollution, and air pollution. The electronic nose (e-nose) and electronic tongue (e-tongue) sense chemicals based on the odor and taste. These sensors can be used to monitor the pollution level and quality of food and agricultural produce.

2.3.5 RADIO FREQUENCY IDENTIFICATION

Radio frequency identification (RFID) is an identification technology. It has a small chip called the RFID tag along with an antenna. Ambient changes in magnetic field are encoded as signals which are then transmitted. These transmitted signals can be read by an RFID reader. When the RFID tag is attached to the object to be tracked, the reader detects and records its presence when the object passes by it.

2.3.6 ACTUATORS

These devices cause changes in the environment by converting the electrical energy into other forms. They include heating or cooling elements, speakers, lights, displays, and motors. In a smart home system, actuators can be used to lock/unlock the doors, switch on/off the lights, control temperature, and notify users.

Consider an operating environment of a mining industry. Such an environment is hazardous. It is essential to monitor the employees closely during their working hours. Sensors can be used to monitor the health of the employees as well as the status of the work. Environmental sensors to detect poisonous gas, ambient temperature, and lighting can be used to warn the employees. Vital signs of the employees can be collected and monitored to find if they are in danger. These sensor details can be analyzed in the local edge at the operation center to ensure the safety of the employees. Edge computing is thus highly beneficial to monitor the safety of the miners.

This section discussed the perceptual component of the edge computing environment. To communicate between various components of the edge computing system an effective communication environment is essential. Section 4 discusses the common network and data protocols that can be used in an edge-computing system. Section 5 discusses the network management using Software-defined networks.

2.4   NETWORKING ARCHITECTURE

IoT devices capture a lot of real-time data in heterogeneous formats. These have to be communicated using suitable communication protocols to the nearby gateways for further processing and transfer of data. The communication protocols can be categorized into two types. The first set consists of network and data link layer protocols [6]. The second category is the data transfer protocols that can be used in the application and session layers (Fig. 2.3). Some of the commonly used network layer protocols [7] include:

- **Bluetooth:** is a secure, short-range, low-power, low-cost, wireless transmission protocol between electronic devices. Data exchange between electronic devices over short distances is facilitated using 2.4 GHz wireless link. Bluetooth star, mesh, and point-to-point topologies are highly suitable for smart home applications.
- **Wi-Fi:** is a family of wireless network protocols, based on the IEEE 802.11 family of standards, which are commonly used for local area networking of devices and Internet access. Any electronic device within range of a wireless modem can attempt to access the network. Sensors in healthcare and smart home applications commonly communicate with the gateway using Wi-Fi.

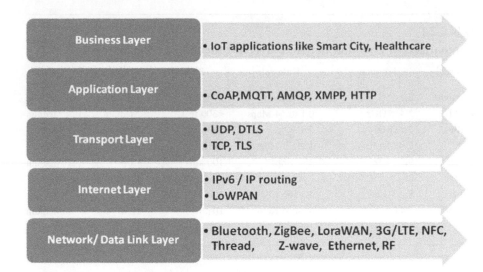

FIGURE 2.3   IoT communication protocols.

- **NFC:** Near-Field Communication is developed by Philips and Sony. It is a very short-range wireless technology that helps devices separated by a few centimeters to communicate based on magnetic field induction. It is used commonly in payments and loyalty points.
- **Zigbee:** based on IEEE 802.15.4 is a cheap low-power, low-bandwidth wireless ad hoc technology for personal area networks. It is commonly used for battery-operated monitoring and control applications.
- **LoRaWAN:** low-power long-range wide area network by Semtech is set up using low radio frequencies (923 MHz in Asia) for up to 10 km range. It helps to setup public or private IoT networks. It can be used in rural areas for water monitoring and management and for smart street lighting applications.
- **LTE:** long-term evolution implements a high-performance air interface for cellular mobile communication systems using radio technologies. Drones can connect to a cellular tower using 4G/LTE.
- **RFID:** radio frequency identification uses wireless electromagnetic fields to identify objects. It is used in manufacturing lines, identification systems, and toll booths. It can be replaced by NFC.
- **Ethernet:** is a wired computer network technology used in LAN, MAN, WAN. *One branch of Ethernet can connect up to* 1,024 nodes. It provides data link and physical layer services.
- **Z-Wave:** works in sub 1 GHz RF band. It is used for low latency, low power applications especially in home automation systems.
- **Thread**: This is an IPv6 protocol based on LowPAN. It complements Wi-Fi technology in home automation. It is an IEEE 802.15.4 based mesh networking protocol. It works in 2.4 GHz frequency and covers a distance of 10–30 m. It can handle up to 250 nodes.

TABLE 2.1
Comparison of common network layer protocols for edge systems

Protocol	Frequency	Data rate	Range	Power usage	Cost
Bluetooth	2.4 GHz	1 to 3 Mbps	300 feet	Low	Low
Wi-Fi	2.4, 5 GHz	0.1 to 54 Mbps	<300 feet	Medium	Medium
ZigBee	2.4 GHz	250 Kbps	300 feet	Low	Medium
LTE	Cellular bands	1 to 10 Mbps	Miles	Medium	High
LoRa	923 MHz	<50 Kbps	100 kms	Low	Medium
RFID	860 to 960 MHz	Up to 100 Mbps	Up to 100 m	Low	High
Z-wave	Sub GHz	40–100 Kbps	100 feet	Low	Medium
Thread	2.4 Ghz	40–250 Kbps	10 m	Low	Medium
NFC	13.56 MHz	106 to 424 kbps	<10 cms	Low	Low

Table 2.1 compares the above-mentioned protocols in terms of frequency, data rate, range of communication, power efficiency, and cost.

Data transfer protocols provide set of rules to establish point-to-point communication with the hardware without Internet connection. It is used for messaging purpose. They provide the rules to define syntax, semantics, error recovery, and data synchronization. Some of the commonly used data protocols include:

- **MQTT:** Message Queue Telemetry Transport is a subscribe/publish protocol layered over Transmission Control Protocol (TCP). This protocol supports event-driven messaging in low-cost, resource-constrained devices. MQTT is used in fire detectors and car sensors. Mosquitto is an open-source MQTT broker.
- **AMQP:** Similar to MQTT, the Advanced Message Queuing Protocol (AMQP) provides a publish/subscribe architecture over TCP. The publisher's messages are received through exchange that distribute them to queues. Queues represent various topics. Listeners subscribe to these topics. When data is available under these topics, subscribers receive the information. It can be used in the device edge to ingest data from various IoT devices.
- **XMPP:** The Extensible Messaging and Presence Protocol was standardized by IETF for message exchange based on publish/subscribe architecture. It uses TCP for transport layer with SSL/TLS based security.
- **CoAP:** The Constrained Application Protocol (CoAP) is an application layer protocol that can be used in resource-constrained wireless sensor network nodes. It has features of HTTP along with multicasting, low overhead, low energy, and simplicity. It is a request-response type of protocol.
- **HTTP:** Hypertext Transfer Protocol is a commonly used Internet protocol in applications like additive manufacturing to connect computers with 3D printers. RESTful architecture is considered for IoT environments. However, HTTP is not preferred due to its cost and energy efficient.

DDS (Data Distribution Service for real-time systems), LLAP (Lightweight Local Automation Protocol), LWM2M (Lightweight M2M), SSI (Simple Sensor Interface) are also commonly used. The next section discusses the importance of automated network management.

2.5 NETWORK MANAGEMENT AND CONTROL

Reconfiguring and managing networking devices like routers and gateways manually is impractical and inefficient due to the following reasons:

- Increase in deployment time and cost.
- Vulnerability to security threats due to proliferation of the IoT devices.
- Hinders production and increases security vulnerabilities due to increase in the downtime of the real-time applications.

This necessitates the use of a good network management solution to install security updates in the devices and applications. A well-controlled network reduces downtime and deployment time of the IoT applications. For this, a technology like software-defined network (SDN) to manage the entire network consistently and holistically is essential. Software-defined networking (SDN) [8] is a networking architecture that enables software applications to programmatically control the network. The layout of the network is configurable dynamically. SDN provides orchestration for network management by decoupling the control plane and the data plane. SDN enables better network management by:

- Facilitating automatic device configuration and bandwidth allocation using virtualization techniques.
- Using security policies and improved access control mechanisms for overcoming the security threats.
- Enabling quick deployment and unified management of all ICT resources.
- Using intelligent techniques for troubleshooting and management of networks.
- Supporting quick and flexible interworking with multiple data platforms and providing capability to collect, analyze, and upload data from IoT devices onto the platform.
- Decoupling of network and data connections facilitates unified data uploading.

Simplified network management with SDN will make IoT systems more reliable, real-time, secure, scalable facilitating unified data management. A layered architecture for network management [9] (Fig. 2.4) using SDN is given below:

Perception layer consists of various devices. Sensors collect data for various applications. Actuators receive commands from the network to perform various tasks.
Communication layer consists of SDN gateways and routers, to transfer data. These gateways are programmatically controlled by the SDN controller. Some of the functionalities of such gateways include data transfer, data storage and processing as

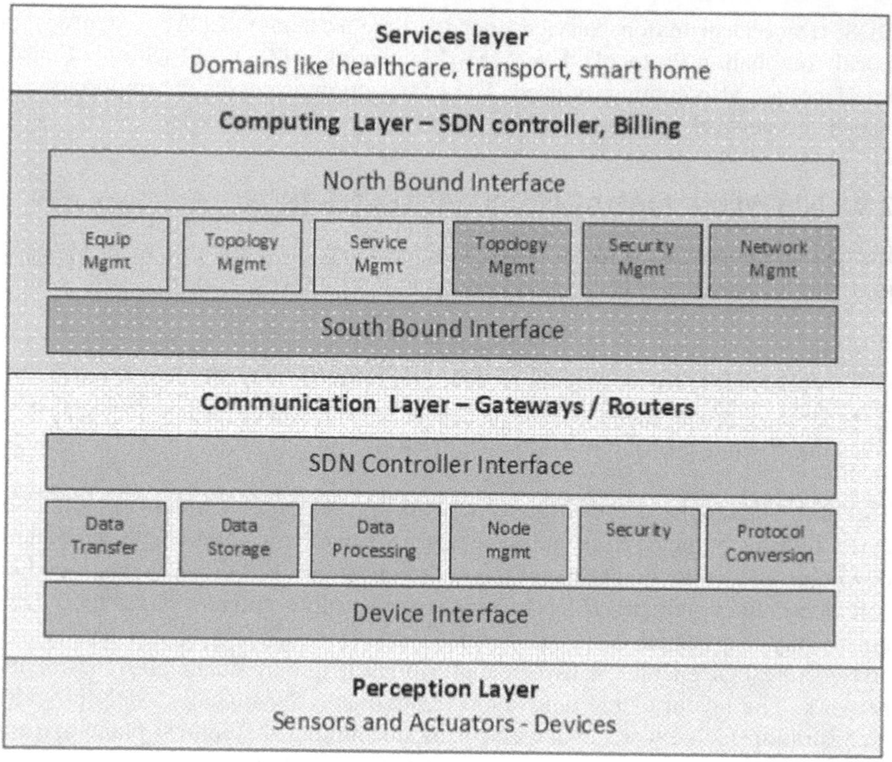

FIGURE 2.4 SDN-based architecture for network management.

directed by the controller. These gateways also perform node management, protocol conversion and security control.

Computing layer contains SDN controller. The controllers control not only data transfer but also process data. Some of the functionalities of the SDN controller include

- Device management that includes configuring, managing of routers/gateways as well as establishment of policies and rules for collection and processing of data in various devices.
- Service management that includes adding or deleting various services and policies supported by gateways and for data management/storage.
- Topology management, that includes routing and topology updation.
- Operation and maintenance of logs, monitoring and managing the functional modules.
- Security management including authentication and access control.
- Network activation using container based virtual network functions.
- Implementation of SDN southbound (SB) and northbound (NB) interfaces.

Northbound interface pass information (rules/services) required from the services layer for controllers to direct gateways/routers. Southbound interface is used to configure routers/gateways and pass the dynamic requests from the controller to communication layer containing routers/gateways.

The edge computing system has heterogeneous pieces of disparate components (hardware and software) that have to be coordinated and managed to complete the task in a unified manner. Section 6 discusses the need for orchestration.

2.5.1 ORCHESTRATION

An Orchestration platform provides a single holistic view of the system by integrating heterogeneous silos of already existing and new IoT systems, software, and devices. It thus enables viewing, monitoring, and automating data management for disparate applications. For example, a logistics company can track a complex, multi-party supply chain, end-to-end. Information stored can be used to analyze shipping conditions and preemptively adjust delivery in case of failure. Some of the advantages of orchestration include:

- Integration of IoT with existing enterprise systems and business logic. In short the platform should have capability to connect heterogeneous sensors, protocols, and software to ensure "connect the unconnected" philosophy of IoT.
- Data unification from existing and new devices and systems.
- Analysis of data from disparate applications. Based on the analysis of historical heterogeneous cross-entity data, suitable actions should be initiated with ease.
- Establishment of connection with various systems in a simple, efficient, and fast manner.
- Configuration of rules with ease.
- Establishment of suitable access control policies among different user groups.

The main objective of this layer is to align the business needs to the disparate applications and data. This layer defines the rules, policies, business logic and automates workflows, resource provisioning, and change management. This layer should be highly scalable to handle the integration. NiFi, Oozie, and Apache Spark are commonly used to ingest, schedule, and process the IoT data in Big Data frameworks like Hadoop.

2.6 EDGE COMPUTING STATE-OF-THE-ART INTERFACES AND DEVICES

2.6.1 MIDDLEWARE

IoT devices are heterogeneous and present in many locations. This necessitates the usage of middleware that can provide services in a transparent manner for the user and enables him to interact with the devices. The middleware abstracts the hardware and provides an application programming interface (API) for communication, data management, computation, security, and privacy. Some of the challenges to be addressed by the middleware include:

- *Interoperability*: Middleware should facilitate collaboration between heterogeneous devices. This includes network, syntactic and semantic interoperability. Network interoperability abstracts the application from various communication protocols. Syntactic interoperability hides various data encoding formats and provides services in a transparent manner to the user. Semantic interoperability ensures transparent interoperability with the domain data.
- *Device discovery and management*: The middleware provides naming service interfaces to list the IoT devices, their services, and capabilities. Based on their capabilities, devices can be discovered. The middle also needs to perform load balancing, power management and error reporting about the devices to the users.
- *Scalability*: Middleware should accommodate changes when device infrastructure scales up or down. Middleware should be able to manage communication between the devices.
- *Security and privacy*: Middleware should be able to manage the privacy and security issues in IoT environment including authentication, user privacy, and access control.
- *Seamless cloud integr*ation: IoT middleware should be able to seamlessly integrate with different types of clouds. This will help the users to analyze data collected from various sensors.
- *Context detection:* Context of the data from various sensors can be used to provide specialized services to users. Context detection aims at collecting data from resources, and selecting the information that can have an impact on the computation. Context based processing uses the gathered information to perform a task or make a decision.

Middleware can be categorized as:

- *Event based*: This type of middleware is based on publish-subscribe architecture. In this model, all the entities interact through events. Each event belongs to a type and is specified with some parameters. Events are generated by producers and received by consumers. Consumer entities can subscribe for events. When such events occur, they get notified by the producers.
- *Service oriented*: This type of middleware abstracts the resources as services provided through a set of interfaces. Service providers publish/advertise their services to repositories. Service consumers then discover the required services from the repository and bind them to access the service. Hydra is a service-oriented middleware with semantic interoperability between services.
- *Database oriented*: This type of middleware abstracts the IoT devices as a virtual centralized relational database system. This system has the advantage of querying the database to extract information. The major issue is scalability due to centralization.

- *Semantic*: This type of middleware enables data exchange between heterogeneous devices. Ontology is used to map different device formats to a common one. A semantic layer maps each resource to a software layer for the resource. The software layers of different resources can now communicate with one another using a common format.
- *Application specific*: The middleware is architected for a specific application. The middleware and application are tightly coupled.

Middleware consists of four functional components to enable abstraction and interoperability among the heterogeneous IoT devices [10] (Fig. 2.5).

- *Interface protocol layer:* This layer enables interoperability between a variety of protocols used in the physical, data link, network, transport, and application layers of the communication stack of an IoT system. For this purpose, a wrapper is placed either in the device side or in the middleware to convert the protocol supported by the device to a common protocol.
- *Device abstraction layer*: This layer enables syntactic and semantic interoperability based on data formats between devices. This layer configures the device profiles and communicates the functionality to them.
- *Context management layer*: IoT devices and middleware should be context-aware. Context-awareness includes context detection and context processing.

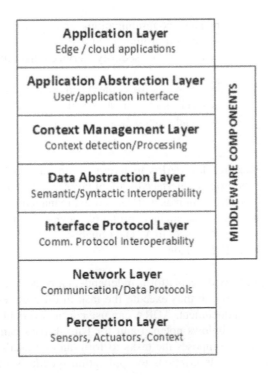

FIGURE 2.5   Middleware functional components.

Context detection involves selecting data collected from the resources based on the computational requirements. Context processing uses this information to make decisions or perform a task.

- *Application abstraction layer*: provides an interface for the applications and end-users to interact with devices. RESTful or query based interfaces can be used.

Middleware solutions address the abstraction and interoperability challenges in IoT environment. Hydra, Aura, TinyDB are some commonly used middleware.

2.6.1.1   Hydra

Hydra is a service oriented middleware. It operates between the applications and operating system layers. The middleware provides a web service interface to interact with the physical devices like sensors, actuators, and transducers transparent to their underlying communication technologies like Bluetooth, RF, ZigBee, RFID, WiFi, etc. Semantic description of these devices is provided through OWL, OWL –S. Each device is considered as a service. The service is exposed through interfaces. User can interact with the devices through these interfaces. Hence the details of the devices including their communication mechanism are abstracted from the users through these interfaces. Hence all the functional components that include protocol, device, syntactic and semantic interoperability are provided by Hydra. The various layers include:

- Network layer to manage communications among heterogeneous devices using various communication protocols. SOAP tunneling can be used.
- Security layer provides various security services like authentication and authorization.
- Semantic services layer provides the context and policy management services.
- Services layer offers services to manage ontology, events, devices, orchestration of jobs, storage, and diagnostics.

2.6.1.2   Aura

Aura aims to provide high-level APIs to interact with various heterogeneous devices. AURA does not provide interface protocol layer and device abstraction layer. It provides application abstraction as well as context management layers. Hence all the functional components that include protocol, device, syntactic and semantic interoperability are provided by AURA. Data analysis capability is also provided. The components of AURA include:

- Task Manager: Provides a platform-independent abstract service for end-users tasks. The end-user can thus execute the task in different environments. For example to edit a document, AURA can use editors available in the operating environment-for windows notepad and for Unix Emacs can be used.
- Service Supplier: composes the tasks to form an end-user's request. It maps the abstract service descriptions to application-specific settings. An abstract

text editor interface may be mapped onto Notepad if Windows environment is used or Emacs if Unix environment is used.

- Context Observer: gathers information about physical context. Different devices have different sensing capabilities. Based on this the context observer gathers information for Task and Environment managers.
- Environment Manager: is knowledgeable of the services provided by the suppliers and their deployment. Based on this knowledge, it maps suitable services to the context observer component.

2.6.1.3 TinyDB

TinyDB middleware enables users to interact with the devices without knowing its specifications. For this purpose, TinyDB provides Domain Specific Language (DSL) for end-users to interact with devices. DSL is a query language that supports selection, join, projection, and aggregation operations. It allows an end-user to get information about the time, place, type, and method of sampling in an embedded sensing environment.

2.6.1.4 FiWare

Context information is collected by FiWare from sensors using REST APIs. Context broker collects this context information and provides facilities to store and query the same. FiWare middleware works on publish-subscribe architecture. Consumers can subscribe to the information published by the brokers. Context adapters act as data transformers for the subscriber. Applications use APIs to query, analyze and mine context information collected by the context broker. Visualization facilities are also provided.

2.6.2 APPLICATION INTERFACES

In previous sections, we have been considering the three major functional components of an IoT system – sensors, communication, and data processing extensively. Information processed in the cloud/edge device has to be delivered to the end-user. This is done with a user interface [3]. The end-user interacts with the system using user interfaces comprising of user screens, web pages, buttons, icons, and forms. Such UI can be used to administer, manage, and control the IoT devices. Configurations for various devices can be provided and managed through a central portal/interface. Each IoT system deployment can also provide a separate interface. The type of interactions that the user can have at the front end with the IoT device depends on the use case. Some common types of interactions include

- Receiving automatic notifications or alerts through SMS, email services.
- Monitoring information from the asset proactively using suitable interfaces for data from the sensors.
- Controlling the IoT system remotely using suitable interfaces for the actuators
- Promoting interoperability with heterogeneous devices, browsers, or operating systems of the end-users.
- Improving the overall experience of the user with the product.

Some of the issues to be considered while designing UIs for IoT include:

- **Simplicity:** The information delivered to the user should be simple and should meet his specific needs. Suitable visualization techniques should be provided to improve understandability of the user.
- **Performance:** As data from IoT devices is voluminous, UI should be designed for scalability. Suitable summarization and visualization techniques should be used to improve the performance of the UI.
- **Sensor connectivity:** Data from sensors may be transferred to the processing applications continuously or in time intervals. Suitable interfaces should be provided to the user to indicate the status of the data transfer.
- **Interoperability:** Capability to connect different UI with heterogeneous sensors.

Front-end technologies commonly used to implement user interfaces include:

- **Angular:** is a JavaScript-based open-source, client-side Web application framework. Developers can create dynamic single-page web applications based on model-view-controller (MVC) architectural pattern and HTML.
- **Node:** is an open-source, cross-platform event-driven runtime environment on the server-side. It is used to build fast, scalable, single-threaded server-side and client-side networking applications.

This chapter had provided an in-depth discussion on various components of an edge computing system including – sensors, networking components including protocols and network management, edge servers, cloud servers, user interfaces, and middleware to support heterogeneity. Creating such a complex edge computing environment is difficult for study purposes. So the following section discusses the simulators.

2.7 EDGE COMPUTING SIMULATORS

Testing solutions in real IoT and edge computing environments is not feasible due to the high cost and diverse domain knowledge required to reason the results. Simulation makes it possible to evaluate the various strategies and algorithms in a repeatable, controlled, and cost-effective way. Tested solutions can then be deployed. There are a number of edge computing simulators [11]. This section discusses the features and architecture of commonly used edge simulators such as PureEdgeSim, iFogSim, and IoTSim-Edge [12].

2.7.1 PureEdgeSim

PureEdgeSim is a java based simulation framework for performance evaluation of cloud, fog, and pure edge computing environments. PureEdgeSim is based on CloudSim. Performance measurement can monitor network usage, latency, resources utilization, and energy consumption. Some of the features of PureEdgeSim include:

- Capability to simulate heterogeneous devices
- Scalability to thousands of devices
- Support for device mobility
- Realistic network, mobility, task generation, and energy models
- Ease of use and visualization
- Support for variety of scenarios related to IoT, VANET, MANET, Clouds, Edge, and Mist computing environments.

Various modules in the PureEdgeSim include:

- *Scenario Manager*: This module loads the user scenario and the simulation parameters. File parser class in the module checks the input files and loads the simulation parameters. Simulation parameters class holds the various parameters.
- *Simulation Manager*: This module initiates simulation, schedules the events, and generates the output. Simulation manager class of this module manages simulation, schedules tasks; while Simulation Logger class generates and saves the simulation output.
- *Data Center Manager*: This module takes care of generating and managing all the data centers and devices. It consists of two classes. The Server Manager class generates the servers and edge devices, their hosts, and virtual machines. The Data Center class maintains the properties of edge devices like location, mobility, energy source, and capacity.
- *Tasks Generator*: This module assigns an application such as e-health, smart-home, and augmented reality to each edge device. Based on the application, tasks are then generated.
- *Network Module*: This module takes care of the transfer of entities like tasks, requests, containers.
- *Tasks Orchestrator*: This module contains the orchestration algorithm defined by the user.
- *Location Manager:* This module generates the mobility path of mobile devices.

2.7.2 IoTSim-Edge

IoTSim-Edge [13] extends the capability of CloudSim to incorporate the different features of edge and IoT devices. Communication among components is handled by the event management system. IoT devices layer simulates different types of IoT devices like sensors for cars, healthcare devices, smart homes, etc. The overall architecture of IoTSim-Edge (Fig. 2.6) is discussed in this paragraph. Data collected by these sensors is processed in edge data center. This edge data center consists of heterogeneous processing devices such as smartphone, laptop, Raspberry Pi or a server. Communication between IoT devices and edge devices is through communication protocols. Heterogeneous network layer and application layer protocols are available. Edge-IoT management layer coordinates processing by receiving user request from users' layer and processing the requests using the

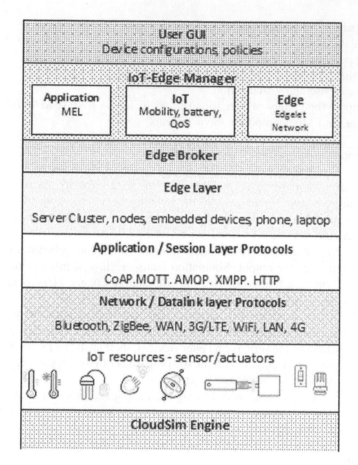

FIGURE 2.6 IoTSim-Edge architecture.

Edge-IoT resources. A graphical user interface (GUI) is used to provide device configuration and policies. Edge-IoT management layer configures Edgelet, policies, mobility, battery, synchronism, QoS and network, communication, transport, and security protocols. An IoT application is represented as a directed acyclic graph (DAG) of MicroElements (MELs). Each MEL abstractly represents the resources, services, and data.

Job submitted/task to be performed by the edge device is called the edgelet. The main classes connected with edge devices include:

- The EdgeDataCenter class establishes connection between edge and IoT devices. This class also performs edge resource provisioning, scheduling, and monitoring edge processing.
- EdgeDataCenter characteristic class maintains the attributes of an EdgeDataCenter like policies, IoT protocols, and IoT devices.
- The EdgeBroker class acts on behalf of users. It initiates the connection establishment between edge and IoT devices through EdgeDataCenter class.

Other functionalities done include negotiating with resources, submitting IoT and edge requests, and receiving results.

- The EdgeDevice class presents the model of edge devices in terms of receiving and processing IoT-generated data based on the EdgeLet policy. Battery class and Moving Policy class give the battery and moving conditions of edge devices like mobile phones.
- The MicroElement (MEL) class models the operation performed on IoT data on edge data centers. The EdgeLet class models tasks that need to be executed inside MEL.

The main classes connected with IoT devices include:

- The IoTdevice class that mimics the behavior of real IoT devices in terms of sensing, processing, mobility, data rate, etc. Since IoT devices are often self-powered and moving, the Battery and Mobility classes exist to empower IoT devices with such characteristics.
- The NetworkProtocol class models the network protocols in terms of speed rate.
- The IoTProtocol class models the features of IoT protocol (like CoAP, XMPP) based on QoS.

UserInterface class provides the necessary methods to easily configure and test the IoT application development without knowing the details of the simulator. It allows a user to define all the parameters using the interactive interface which is converted to the desired configuration file.

Workflow for task execution in IoTSim-Edge (Fig. 2.7) is given below:

- IoT-Edge environment is initialized. IoT application given by the user communicates with the EdgeBroker.
- Edge Broker starts the IoT devices and connects to them.
- Edge Broker then instructs EdgeDataCenter to connect IoT devices to MEL.
- The IoT devices are notified once connected.
- An IoT device senses and generates an edgelet (Task).
- IoT device can perform preliminary processing on edgelet like filtering based on the resources.
- IoT device sends the edgelet to the IoT broker.

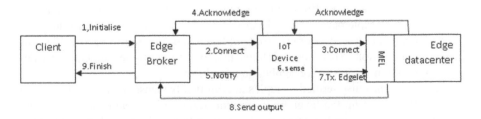

FIGURE 2.7 Workflow.

- IoT broker submits the IoT edgelet data to MEL in edge data center.
- MEL processes the data and sends results to IoT Broker.
- The attributes of IoT devices like battery consumption and location are continuously monitored by the EdgeDataCenter.
- IoT broker then reports to the user.

2.7.3 iFogSim

Fog is an intermediate layer between the user and remote (public) cloud. This layer is closer to the user than the cloud. Hence the performance of the networking environment can be improved. Edge computing has programmable systems. It is usually at the location of the end-user. Mist layer is a computing platform between edge devices and fog layer. Edge computing can work without a fog layer.

iFogSim is an event-based simulator for edge, fog, and IoT environments [14]. It uses CloudSim to handle events of various components. The following are the classes of iFogSim that are required to simulate the fog network:

- Fog device
- Sensor
- Actuator
- Tuple
- Application
- Monitoring edge
- Resource management service

iFogSim has a layered architecture (Fig. 2.8) consisting of:

- *Device layer* comprises IoT sensors and actuators that act as source or sink of data. Sensors emit data with certain attributes including time or size of emission. Network characteristics include latency, bandwidth, etc. This layer is implemented using sensor and actuator classes. Sensor class maintains attributes that characterize the camera or the temperature sensor along with its network capability and data generated. Actuator class characterizes the actuator along with data received from the fog devices and mode of actuation.
- *Fog device* can host application modules. Gateways are fog devices that connect IoT devices with the network. Fog layer can also host private cloud in between the public cloud and devices layer. The resources are arranged in a hierarchical fashion. Offloading computation can be from a lower to a higher level. It is implemented using FogDevice class that maintains attributes like memory, processor, storage size, uplink, and downlink bandwidths for communication. This class contains methods to schedule, allocate and decommission resources for application modules.
- *Data Streams* also termed as tuples are emitted by sensors and fog devices to be transferred up the layer for communication. Data streams are also transmitted from an application module to an actuator. It is implemented using

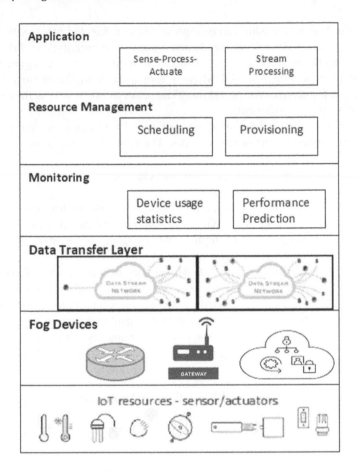

FIGURE 2.8 Architecture of iFogSim.

tuple class characterized by its type and the source and destination application modules. It includes the length of data in tuple and processing requirements.

- *Monitoring layer* keeps track of the resource usage, power consumption, and device/resource availability. The output of this layer is used by the resource management layer. Each device maintains its usage statistics and reports to the monitoring layer. This layer also predicts a device performance. The executeTuple() method in the FogDevice class contains the tuple processing logic where the device updates its resource use. These statistics can also be encapsulated in a tuple and sent to the resource management layer.
- *Resource management layer* is used to manage various resources. It identifies the resources (fog/IoT layer devices) to be allocated to a particular application based on its static QoS requirements. Resource allocation can be centralized, distributed, or hybrid.
- *Application (programming) models.* An application is modeled as a collection of modules. These modules can generate data that can be used by another

module. This relationship can be represented as a directed graph with vertices forming the modules and the directed edges representing the flow of information between the modules. Processing models can be categorized as

- Sense-process-actuate model where information from the sensors is transmitted to fog devices for processing. The result of processing is then used for actuating the environment.
- Stream-processing model. A cluster of fog devices process real-time data streams emitted by the sensor devices. The result is stored in the fog layer.

This layer is implemented using the following classes:

- AppModule class maintains the processing elements of fog applications. It realizes the vertices of the DAG. An *AppModule* instance processes a coming tuple and generates output tuples that are sent to the next modules in the DAG.
- AppEdge class maintains the data dependency between a pair of application modules. Each edge is characterized by the type of tuple it carries, which is captured by the *TupleType* attribute of AppEdge class along with the processing requirements and length of data encapsulated in these tuples.
- An AppLoop instance specifies application loops given by the user. It contains a list of modules starting from the origin of the loop to the module where the loop terminates.

2.7.3.1   Creating Topology and Executing an Application in iFogSim Simulator

Topology creation and execution on iFogSim is elaborated in this section

- Install Eclipse IDE
- Download and unzip iFogSim from CloudsLab link
- Create a java project in Eclipse IDE, add FogSim path
- Under src → org.fog.gui.example → FogGui.java and run as java application. Fog Topology creator is opened. New topology can be created or an existing topology can be opened by importing.
- Consider a case of video monitoring. Cameras are sensors. Based on the analysis of images sensed by the cameras, actuators initiate actions. Four sensors and four actuators are initialized. The images scanned by the cameras are used for motion detection, user interface, object detection, and object tracking. Motion detection is done in the IoT-Device, while, other actions are done in the fog device/cloud. A gateway is setup between the IoT and Cloud layers. The area is divided into two areas, each with two sensors and two actuators. The topology is created in the Topology creator and saved.

While creating the topology, either a fog device or an edge device (sensor or actuator) can be selected. When a fog device is selected attributes like name, type, uplink, downlink, MIPS, RAM, and rate have to be given. When sensor is selected, name, type, signal – deterministic, normal, or uniform distribution with parameters have to be entered. For actuators, name and type have to be entered. Then links between the devices are to be created with latency by choosing the link icon. The topology generated is shown in Fig. 2.9. As the topology is created, the corresponding console-generated message is shown in Fig. 2.10.

On execution of the java application. The details (Fig. 2.11) showing establishment of connections, execution of application, and energy consumption are displayed in Eclipse console.

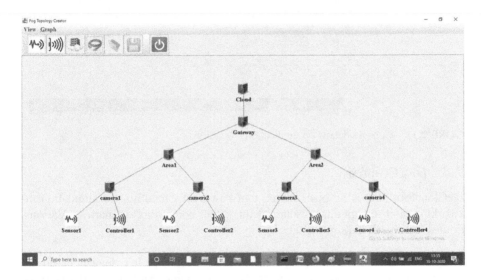

FIGURE 2.9 Topology creation.

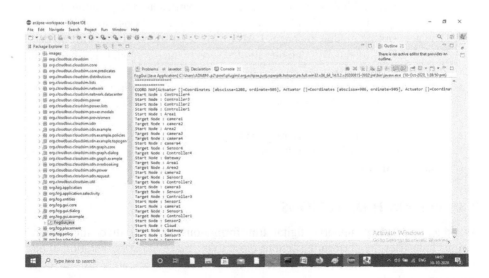

FIGURE 2.10 Console details when topology is created.

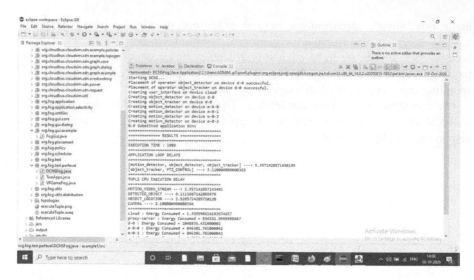

FIGURE 2.11   Console details on application execution.

2.7.4   EDGECLOUDSIM

EdgeCloudSim [15] is an open source tool based on CloudSim for simulation of networking and computing resources for edge computing scenarios. Various Modules in EdgeCloudSim include:

- Mobility Module that manages the location of mobile IoT devices based on updating their x and y coordinates in a hash table. Mobility model class is used. Inbuilt model is nomadic mobility model.
- Load Generator Module: generates tasks for a particular configuration. By default task generation models Poisson distribution in LoadGeneratorModel class.
- The networking module manages LAN/WAN network parameters for upload/ download of data. By default single server queue model is inbuilt in NetworkModel class.
- Edge Orchestrator Module: decides the resources to handle incoming client requests. A probabilistic handler is inbuilt in the EdgeOrchestrator class for this purpose.
- Core Simulation Module is responsible for loading and running the Edge Computing scenarios from the configuration files. It also saves results of execution in a file.

2.8   RESEARCH DIRECTIONS

As edge computing supports digital transformation and data diversification of various industries, by performing actions close to the place of data generation, it has become a hot research topic. Some of the directions for research [16] in edge computing include:

Computation offloading: As IoT devices are resource constrained, more complex computations are usually performed in remote clouds. To minimize network transfer latency, computations can be offloaded into devices and resources at the edge of the network. Hence computation offloading, is the main drive behind edge computing and is highly related to task scheduling. In edge computing, the application can be executed locally in the device or partially or fully offloaded and executed in the resources available at the network edge. Various system parameters like bandwidth, size of the data, and energy consumed are monitored. Based on the resource availability, decision engine can predict the task execution and suitable resources will be allocated based on the metrics like latency and energy consumption. Computation offloading is an active area of research.

Resource allocation: Once offloading decision is made, the computing tasks should be allocated to suitable resources. If the subtasks of a job are highly related and indivisible, then they are allocated to the same resource at the edge. Otherwise these subtasks can be executed on multiple resources on different nodes. Optimal and intelligent resource allocation based on storage, computing, network and an energy requirement of the tasks is an active research area.

Mobility management: Edge computing mainly aims at allocating edge resources close to devices to offload computations. If devices are static then edge resources can be identified statically. If devices are mobile, dynamic resource discovery and low latency resource switching are essential to ensure service continuity. Mobility based service migration prediction technique is used to balance cost with service delivery.

Traffic offloading: Like computation offloading, based on the latency, bandwidth, localization, energy and other network, traffic can be offloaded at the edge of the network. The main objective is to offload computations in a manner to reduce network congestion.

Caching: Caching techniques enable efficient content distribution and improve the user experience. Content caching at the edge of the network avoid repeated data transfer, network congestion and traffic. Cache location and cache management policies is a hot research topic.

Network control: Programmatically controlling the networks in the edge computing system using software defined networks is an active research area.

Data security and privacy: The distributed architecture of edge computing makes it vulnerable to malware infections and security breaches. Some of hot research topics include light weight encryption techniques to suite the resource constraints of the devices. This ensures security of data in transfer. Further, when data is stored suitable techniques for secure data storage is essential. Homomorphic encryption can be used for searchable encryption. This ensures security as well as performance. Data security is ensured using suitable confidentiality and integrity techniques. Proposing suitable authentication and access control mechanisms for individuals and groups suited to the resource constraints and distributed nature of edge computing systems. Authentication mechanisms include individual, cross domain and handover authentication while migrating from one domain to another. Access control mechanisms include attribute-based and role-based approaches. Preserving individual privacy using suitable privacy preservation techniques. The privacy problems in the edge computing environment involve establishing a trade-off between

- Data outsourcing through computation offloading and maintaining data privacy.
- Offering location based service and maintaining data privacy.
- Data sharing and preserving individual privacy.

One of the most researched area is integrating blockchain with edge computing systems. It is a mutually beneficial integration. Blockchain offers security including confidentiality and integrity while preserving privacy of data in edge computing environment that is heterogeneous and scalable. Edge computing offers required resources for the blockchain environment.

2.9 SUMMARY

Edge computing is a distributed computing paradigm that offloads device computation to network edge like a building. It reduces latency and performs computation close to the end devices. This chapter discussed the need for edge computing in an industrial environment. The detailed architecture of an edge computing environment with the functionality of various components was discussed in this chapter. Device and local edge nodes to perform computation at network edge improve the effectiveness of the application based on the availability of the resources. Devices, networks, and computation resources form the core of the edge computing system. Sensors and actuators perceive the environment. Various communication protocols including networking protocols and data transfer protocols were discussed in detail. Network management is essential to configure and maintain the disparate resources and enable communication between them. For this purpose automated network management using SDN was discussed. As the edge computing environment is highly heterogeneous, middleware is required to integrate these entities to function as a unified whole. Further, a suitable interface is required to interact with the user. This chapter provided a detailed discussion on middleware architecture and need for user interfaces. As the system is highly complex, it is difficult to build a real edge computing system to test an application. So simulators are used. This chapter gives a detailed discussion on features and architecture of various simulators such as IoTSim-Edge, iFogSim, and EdgeSim. Steps to set up topology and execute an application on iFogSim was also provided. Finally, the chapter concluded with pointers to possible directions for research in the area of edge computing.

REFERENCES

1. Shi, W., Cao, J., Zhang, Q., Li, Y., & Xu, L. (2016, October).Edge computing: Vision and challenges. *IEEE Internet of Things Journal*, 3(5), 637–646. doi: 10.1109/JIOT. 2016.2579198.
2. Singh Dikhit, R. (2018, March 27). All about edge computing architecture, open source frameworks and IoT solutions. *OpenSource*.
3. Satyanarayanan, M. (2017, January). The emergence of edge computing. *Computer*, 50(1), 30–39. doi: 10.1109/MC.2017.9.
4. Ai, Y., Peng, M., & Zhang, K. (2018). Edge computing technologies for Internet of Things: A primer. *Digital Communications and Networks*, 4(2), 77–86. ISSN 2352-8648, https://doi.org/10.1016/j.dcan.2017.07.001.
5. Sunyaev, A. (2020). Fog and edge computing. In: Sunyaev, A. (ed) *Internet computing*, Springer, Cham, 10.1007/978-3-030-34957-8_8.

6. Anawar, M. R., Wang, S., Zia, M. A., Khan Jadoon, A., Akram, U., & Raza, S.(2018). Fog computing: An overview of big IoT Data analytics. *Wireless Communications and Mobile Computing*, *2018*, 22. 10.1155/2018/7157192.

7. Al-Sarawi, S., Anbar, M., Alieyan, K., & Alzubaidi, M. (2017). Internet of Things (IoT) communication protocols: Review. In *Proc. 2017 8th International Conference on Information Technology (ICIT)*, Amman, 685–690. doi: 10.1109/ICITECH.2017. 8079928.

8. Taherizadeh, S., Jones, A. C., Taylor, I., Zhao, Z., Stankovski, V. (2018). Monitoring self-adaptive applications within edge computing frameworks: A state-of-the-art review. *Journal of Systems and Software*, *136*, 19–38. ISSN 0164-1212, 10.1016/j.jss. 2017.10.033.

9. Latif, Z., Sharif, K., Li, F., Karim, M. M., Biswas, S., & Wang, Y. (2020). A comprehensive survey of interface protocols for software defined networks. *Journal of Network and Computer Applications*, *156*, 102563. ISSN 1084-8045, 10.1016/j.jnca. 2020.102563.

10. Sethi, P., & Sarangi, S. R. (2017). Internet of things: Architectures, protocols, and applications. *Journal of Electrical and Computer Engineering*, *2017*, 25. 10.1155/ 2017/9324035.

11. Ashouri, M., Lorig, F., Davidsson, P., & Spalazzese, R. (2019). Edge computing simulators for IoT system design: An analysis of qualities and metrics. *Future Internet*, *11*, 235.

12. Gupta, H., et al. (2017). iFogSim: A toolkit for modeling and simulation of resource management techniques in the Internet of Things, Edge and Fog computing environments. *Software: Practice and Experience*, *47*, 1275–1296.

13. Jha, D. N., Alwasel, K., Alshoshan, A., Huang, X., Naha, R. K., Battula, S. K., Garg, S., Puthal, D., James, P., Zomaya, A. Y., Dustdar, S., & Ranjan, R. (2020). IoTSim-Edge: A simulation framework for modeling the behaviour of IoT and Edge Computing environments. *Software: Practice and Experience*, *2020*, 1–23.

14. Sonmez, C., Ozgovde, A., & Ersoy, C. (2017). EdgeCloudSim: An environment for performance evaluation of Edge Computing systems. In *Proc. 2017 Second International Conference on Fog and Mobile Edge Computing (FMEC)*, Valencia, 39–44. doi: 10.1109/FMEC.2017.7946405.

15. Perez Abreu, D., Velasquez, K., Curado, M., & Monteiro, E. (2020). A comparative analysis of simulators for the Cloud to Fog continuum. *Simulation Modelling Practice and Theory*, *101*, 102029. ISSN 1569-190X, 10.1016/j.simpat.2019.102029.

16. Cao, K., Liu, Y., Meng, G., & Sun, Q. (2020). An overview on edge computing research. *IEEE Access*, *8*, 85714–85728. doi: 10.1109/ACCESS.2020.2991734.

3 Edge Analytics

3.1 TYPES OF DATA

In statistics, the data are classified into two categories: quantitative and qualitative as represented in Fig. 3.1. The quantitative data is also called as numerical data that deals with numbers and things that can be measured. For example, height, weight, age, price, temperature, humidity, etc. It is then sub-classified into discrete and continuous data. Discrete information holds only finite number of possible values where it is counted using the whole numbers. For example, number of persons standing in the queue (i.e. 26 persons). The continuous information holds infinite number of probable values that lie in a specific range. For example, weight of the persons standing in the queue (i.e. 49.5 kilograms).

The qualitative data is also called as categorical data that are not numerical data rather it is defined using natural language specifications. For example, persons gender, place of birth, language, occupation, etc. In some cases, it also takes on numerical values (i.e. 1 for true and 0 for false) but it does not have mathematical meaning to it. The qualitative data is then sub-classified into nominal and ordinal data where nominal values represent discrete units and have no quantitative order among the values. For example, the languages learned by a student. (i.e. English, Tamil, Hindi, French, German). The ordinal data deals with discrete and ordered units. For example, participant feedback on the workshop attended (i.e. Excellent-4, Good-3, Satisfactory-2, Not satisfactory-1).

Type of the data is significant because data analysis for continuous values works differently than categorical values. If it is not handled with care it will result in a wrong analysis. Thus understanding the nature of data helps in choosing the correct data analytic method for analysis.

3.2 DATA ANALYTICS

The data analytics implies the process of exploring datasets to bring implications about the information they hold. Data analytic techniques take raw data and expose its patterns to mine knowledge out of it. Further, the analysis is used to produce graphical reports and dashboards as an end result. Data analytics handles data to generate the pattern and produce reports for analysis (Fig. 3.2).

3.3 GOALS OF DATA ANALYTICS

Data analytics adds a huge significance to diverse domains and businesses, where it helps uncover the end result of almost all complex queries from a huge data set, also it can predict the future which would help make business decisions more accurately at appropriate time. Data analytics integrated with Internet of Things (IoT) accelerates

DOI: 10.1201/9781003230946-3

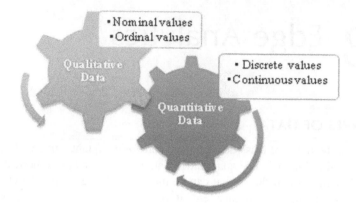

FIGURE 3.1 Types of data.

Data collection   Analysis   Report

FIGURE 3.2 Flow of data analytics.

the current business models to behave still smarter [2]. Meanwhile, the importance of data analytics in varied disciplines includes following generic objectives:

- To find newer opportunities and trends
- To make right decisions at right time
- To increase the satisfaction of the customers
- To reduce energy, cost, and manpower
- To optimize the performance, inventory and increase productivity
- To manage risk and fraud detection
- To be superior among the competitors

3.4 DOMAINS BENEFITING FROM BIG DATA ANALYTICS

The data analysis plays a vital role in various domains for implementing distinct applications [2]. The domains include:

- Healthcare
- Science and research
- E-commerce
- Machine performance

- Business, customer, and personal insight
- Retail management and solutions
- Image processing
- Natural language processing
- Smart city applications
- Smart home applications
- Banking, Insurance, and Finance
- Sports
- Automotive
- Risk management
- Marketing and advertisement
- Disaster forecasting
- Gaming
- Logistics
- Robotics
- Security

3.5   REAL-TIME APPLICATIONS OF DATA ANALYTICS

Some of the applications of data analytics are as follows:

- Predicting the price of a mobile phone based on its specifications such as RAM, screen size, battery capacity, processor, camera, operating system, brand, weight, color, and so on.
- Recommending movies based on the similarity of the ones that have been watched previously by the users.
- Analyzing the customer opinion on the product based on its reviews.
- Diagnosing the disease of a patient by analyzing the symptoms they possess.

3.6   PHASES OF DATA ANALYTICS

The general phases in data analytics are:

- Data collection and pre-processing
- Machine learning-model building
- Performance evaluation

3.6.1   DATA COLLECTION AND PRE-PROCESSING

At the initial stage of data analytics life cycle as shown in Fig. 3.3, stakeholders analyze the business trends and domain of the project they would start to build a hypothesis for resolving the business problems. They will start observing the dataset for identifying key variables and categorizing the values in the dataset. When the nature of the data is understood, stakeholder prepares the data by removing duplicates, replacing missing values and handling noises in the dataset. This phase helps cleanse the data as per the data analytics requirement [6].

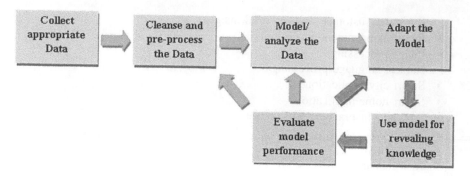

FIGURE 3.3 Data analytics life cycle.

3.6.2 MACHINE LEARNING-MODEL BUILDING

The team with stakeholders, after pre-processing the data, starts building the learning model after identifying the techniques and methods predominantly for dealing with the critical business crisis. The models are nothing but a mix of machine learning algorithms, statistical and mathematical computations performed on the data to attain the expected goal. General machine learning procedure deals with the following terms:

> Labeled data: Data that holds a label/tag which represents its class/category.
> Unlabeled data: Data does not hold a label/tag to represent its class/category.
> Features: These are the columns in the dataset/table.
> Training: The dataset is divided into training and testing sets in the ratio of user's choice. (i.e. 70% for training and 30% for testing). Model is trained with the extracted features of training dataset.
> Validation: The training set can then be split into training and validation set. Validation is a phase that helps in providing most optimized model by changing hyper-parameters based on the validation test results.
> Testing: Machine learning model is modeled to predict the result for test dataset.

Machine learning algorithms are classified into the following categories based on its capability to handle labeled/unlabeled data.

Supervised Learning

Supervised learning is a machine learning technique that handles well labeled/tagged data to train the machine as shown in Fig. 3.4. Here the system requires a supervisor which is the training dataset as the machine learns from it. Supervised learning algorithms then are grouped into the following subgroups.

1. **Regression**: The regression technique helps predict the value of dependent variable "Y" with respect to the single independent variable "X" or multiple independent variables "X1, X2 …. Xn".

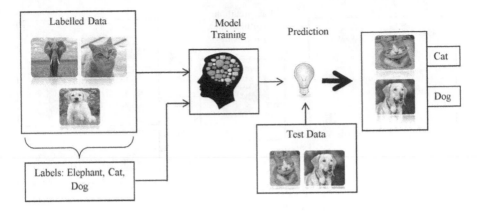

FIGURE 3.4 Supervised learning mechanism.

2. **Classification:** By using the classification technique, the machine is trained to categorize the value into specific class.

Some Popular Supervised Learning Algorithms

- Linear Regression for Regression Problem
- Logistic Regression for Classification Problem
- K-Nearest Neighbors for Classification Problem
- Support Vector Machine Classification Problem
- Random Forest for Classification and Regression Problems

Application: Consider the dataset consisting of objects such as lion, tiger, and dog with the category tagged in every object and it is used to train a model to recognize new input objects.

Unsupervised Learning

Unsupervised learning is a machine learning technique that acquires inferences from the dataset where the values are unlabeled/not tagged [8]. The system does not require any supervisor for learning. The machine acquires knowledge through observation and gets trained as depicted in Fig. 3.5.

Unsupervised learning algorithms then are grouped into following subgroups.

1. **Clustering:** It is an unsupervised machine learning technique that segregates sample space into various cluster groups by discovering similarities between the individuals. This technique uses input values alone to predict patterns and anomalies with respect to similarities. Various distance calculation techniques such as Euclidian distance, Manhattan distance are involved in finding the similarity/dissimilarity among the objects.
2. **Association:** It is an unsupervised machine learning technique that helps identifying the probability of relationships among values. These techniques are widely used for finding sales correlation in transactional data.

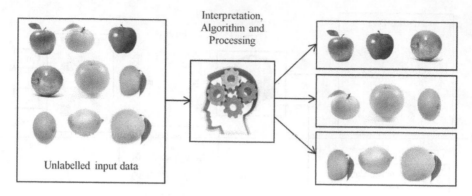

FIGURE 3.5   Unsupervised learning mechanism.

Some Popular Unsupervised Learning Algorithms

- Hierarchical Clustering
- K-Means clustering
- K-Nearest Neighbor Clustering
- Principal Component Analysis
- Singular Value Decomposition
- Independent Component Analysis
- Apriori Algorithm

Applications

In retail markets, retailers discover the relationship between items by analyzing previous transactions to uncover associations among them. By analyzing purchase history, the combination of items that occur more frequently is identified and kept closer to improve sales of products.

Semi-Supervised Learning

This problem relies upon supervised and unsupervised techniques. In this case, some data in the dataset is labeled and rest of the other data is not labeled. To resolve this kind of problem combination of both supervised and unsupervised learning algorithms can be used. The flow of the process is depicted in Fig. 3.6.

Applications

Photo archive with few images tagged with its category and many are not. Unsupervised technique can be used to discover the pattern over the dataset or supervised learning technique can be used to guess the unlabeled values then the same dataset can be feedback to the supervised model as training data.

Reinforcement Learning

Reinforcement learning is a machine learning method that facilitates an agent to gain knowledge of a situation on a trial and error basis. Supervised learning maps labeled input to the output and unsupervised learning is to determine the similarity

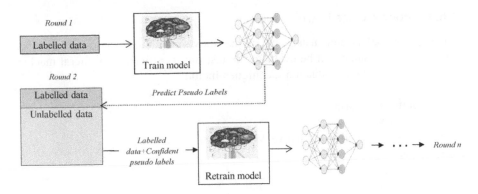

FIGURE 3.6   Semi supervised learning mechanism.

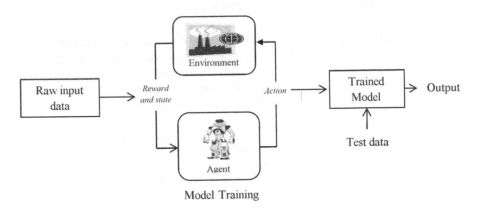

FIGURE 3.7   Reinforcement learning mechanism.

among data points to classify it. Whereas, the reinforcement learning make use of rewards and punishments based strategy for positive and negative actions respectively. The goal of this system is to determine the behavior model that gains the maximum total cumulative reward. This process flow is shown in Fig. 3.7.

Some Popular Reinforcement Learning Algorithms

- Markov Decision Process (MDP)
- Q-Learning
- State-Action-Reward-State-Action(SARSA)
- Deep Q-Networks (DQN)
- Deep Deterministic Policy Gradient (DDPG)

Applications

In robotics field, gaming and engineering automation, reinforcement learning are used to facilitate the agent to produce well-organized control structure which gains knowledge from its own actions and performances.

3.6.3 PERFORMANCE EVALUATION

When the model is built using any of the above-mentioned algorithms, the performance of the same will be evaluated to test out its efficiency. General machine learning performance evaluation techniques include,

- Confusion matrix
- Accuracy
- Precision/ Positive Predictive Value(PPV)
- Recall
- F1 score
- Specificity
- Negative Predictive Value(NPV)
- PR curve
- Receiver Operating Characteristics(ROC) curve

In order to understand the evaluation techniques, let's consider an example scenario where the task is to identify whether patient is having corona disease (reports positive) or is found healthy(reports negative). In general, the results of this classification problem fall into one among the four categories such as True Positive, True Negative, False Positive, and False Negative as depicted in Table 3.1.

True Positive (TP): The patient is corona positive and predicted positive
True Negative (TN): The patient is corona negative and predicted negative
False Positive (FP): The patient is corona negative and predicted positive
False Negative (FN): The patient is corona positive and predicted negative

Confusion Matrix

Confusion matrix is a matrix visualization of the classification results in terms of the parameters TP, TN, FP, and FN.

Accuracy

Accuracy is a metric to evaluate model performance based on its accurate predictions. The formula for calculating accuracy is the correct predictions upon the total predictions.

TABLE 3.1

Confusion matrix – actual versus predicted values

		Predicted	
		Negative	**Positive**
Actual	Negative	*True Positive*	*False Negative*
	Positive	*False Positive*	*True Negative*

$$\text{Accuracy} = \frac{TP + TN}{TP + TN + FP + FN} \tag{3.1}$$

This metric might be deceptive when there are only positive cases in the dataset and the model has classified everything correct and produced 100% accuracy. But still it failed to check negative cases when the model is not capable to classify them. This is called as Accuracy Paradox. So when the classes are imbalanced, accuracy metric might be misleading.

Precision

Precision is an evaluation metric that focuses on finding the percentage of actual positive cases in the total predicted positive cases. It is also called as positive predictive value (PPV).

$$\text{Precision} = \frac{TP}{TP + FP} \tag{3.2}$$

Recall

Recall is an evaluation metric that aims at determining the valid positive cases in the total available positive cases so as to identify the other missed positive cases. Recall is also termed as Sensitivity, Hit Rate or True Positive Rate (TPR).

$$\text{Recall} = \frac{TP}{TP + FN} \tag{3.3}$$

F1 Score

When the cost of False Positive and False Negative is high in an application, Precision and Recall are used to be the superior metrics respectively. It is trusted that F1 score is a better evaluation metric as it computes harmonic mean of Precision and Recall. Also, when there is an imbalanced class distribution, the F1 score is considered as a better option. As it provides weightage for both precision and recall.

$$\text{F1} - \text{score} = 2 * \frac{\text{Recall} * \text{Precision}}{\text{Recall} + \text{Precision}} \tag{3.4}$$

Specificity

Specificity is an evaluation metric that calculates the proportion of correctly predicted negative cases in the overall available negative cases so as to identify the other missed negative instances in the result.

$$\text{Specificity} = \frac{TN}{TN + FP} \qquad (3.5)$$

The False Positive Rate (FPR) is calculated using the specificity value.

$$\text{FPR} = 1 - \text{Specificity} \qquad (3.6)$$

Negative Predictive Value

Negative Predictive Value (NVP) is a metric that focuses on finding the proportion of the valid negative cases in the predicted negative cases.

$$\text{Negative Predictive Value} = \frac{TN}{TN + FN} \qquad (3.7)$$

PR Curve

PR Curve is a graph representation of Recall and Precision values in x and y-axis respectively. It is significant that an algorithm must have high precision and high recall values. An efficient PR Curve is the one which has greater area under curve (AUC).

Receiver Operating Characteristics (ROC) curve

ROC curve is a graph plot between True Positive Rate (TPR) and False Positive Rate (FPR). In other terms, it visualizes the relationship between sensitivity and 1-Specificity in y and x-axis respectively. The larger the Area under the ROC curve, the more accurate the model will be.

3.7 TYPES OF DATA ANALYTICS

In general, data analytics techniques are classified into four types based on its purpose of exploiting the model: descriptive analytics, diagnostic analytics, predictive analytics, and prescriptive analytics. It is depicted in Fig. 3.8.

3.7.1 DESCRIPTIVE ANALYTICS

Descriptive analytics expresses an outline of an action that has happened in the past. This category of analytics is useful in interpreting the pattern from previous actions and it results in data visualizations like charts, graphs, reports, and dashboards. In order to that, enhanced approaches for the future can be framed. It analyses the data in such a way that it would provide appropriate answer for the question "What happened in the past?"

For example, the business organizations analyses and provide a historic review of sales and advertisements.

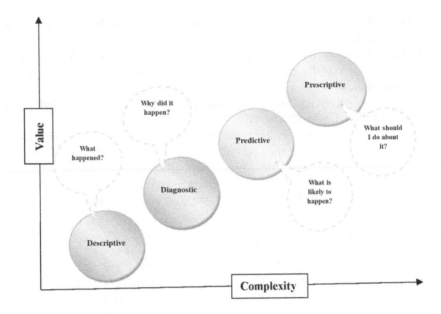

FIGURE 3.8   Types of data analytics.

3.7.2   DIAGNOSTIC ANALYTICS

Diagnostic analytics provides broader insight of an issue as it is a successor to the descriptive analytics. This category of analytics is helpful to mine deeper into a concern in order to identify the source of the problem. Diagnostic analytics also called as root cause analysis. It aims at providing an answer to the question "Why something happened?"

For example, in healthcare domain, when more number of patients are admitted unusually in the hospitals, the diagnostic analytics would bring a root cause of the scenario by analyzing symptoms of all the patients to provide a reason over the unexpected raise in the patient volume.

3.7.3   PREDICTIVE ANALYTICS

Predictive analytics utilizes the key observations of descriptive, diagnostic analytics and various tools and techniques to discover classes and outliers in the system in order to forecast upcoming trend based on the current actions. It aims at providing an answer to the question "What is likely to happen?"

For example, power plants can trim down unanticipated machine failures by predicting when equipment might fall short. Therefore, helping to decrease maintenance expenses and improve resource accessibility.

3.7.4   PRESCRIPTIVE ANALYTICS

The main idea of prescriptive analytics is to recommend the action to avoid upcoming problems or to completely acquire the benefits of current trend. It analyses the data in such a way that it provides appropriate answer for the question "What should I do about it?"

For example, the Ola cab finds the optimal route from source to destination by considering the minimal distance and traffic out of all available paths to make use of the resource efficiently.

In the Data Analytics taxonomy, the most thriving area called Edge Analytics will be a Game Changer!

An edge device is any type of hardware that manages transmission of data at the border line connecting two separate network groups. It accomplishes different roles such as communication, monitoring, processing, filtering, and optimal direction-finding based on the kind of device that is located at the edge. But basically, they act as an extremity of a network through which the data could enter/exit [7].

3.8 EDGE DATA ANALYTICS

Experience Notes: Data is precious and we are surrounded with data everywhere. The most valuable asset in the world is data but 90% of the data is left out without being processed properly. Through effective analysis of data we can detect any kind of patterns. The data contains answers for all our queries but in a hidden way. To extract the required information from the enormous data that evolve around us a proper system should be in place which connects and analyses the data to provide us the info what we need. Edge analytics combining with ML is all to play here for. The world is moving toward in demand of real experience in all means. For example, it can be for buying a product or statistical analysis on user experience or trend analysis or decision systems, etc. Assessing the data in all dimensions and visualizing the same to have a better decision system is in need of time. Without edge analytics, this would not be complete.

To put it in simple words as said by various experts edge analytics is performing the analysis at the point where the data is getting generated. For example traffic system, whereby performing the dynamic analysis information can be sent to the nearby police officials on any trouble in the surrounding. Machine learning models to be created with proper filtering conditions for an effective dynamic learning. For a decisive system to be very effective, model has to be trained in an unsupervised fashion (dynamically) and combination of edge analytics with machine learning is the need of the hour. This unit explains and covers the same which will for sure a clear gateway for the aspiring ones in the field of edge analytics involving machine learning.

—Dr. C.S. Saravana Kumar, Software Architect, Robert Bosch, India.

Edge analytics is the process of gathering, dealing out, and analyzing of data either at the edge of a network or closer to a network connecting device or at some other edge processing software installed nearby. With the advancements of IoT and connecting devices in automating the systems, several industries for instance healthcare, energy, automotive and manufacturing are producing huge amount of data at the edge of the network. Earlier approaches were collecting these data and stored them on cloud or data centers for further processing. As the size of data increases, time taken to push the data to centralized platform and processing them consumes more quantity of time [5]. The objective here is, to process and analyze the data between the actual source of the data and the data center. It is an optimized and distributed mechanism to IoT and cloud computing systems that reduce latency also decision making will be on time. Processing devices at the edge permit data to be analyzed and the reports are to be distributed to ultimate user for preventing breakdowns in well-timed manner. These edge analytics could be of type descriptive or diagnostic or predictive analytics depending on the requirement of an application [8].

It is extremely essential to be aware of where edge data analytics suits the most!

Monitoring the systems for real-time safety is crucial for decisive infrastructures such as oil rigs, gas, aircraft, and CCTV cameras [1]. In order to safeguard these critical systems from any kind of disasters many smart devices and functionalities are being developed. Edge analytics is one of such solutions that detects the malfunctions at the earlier stage and alarms the respective personnel to act accordingly.

Let's consider a scenario of an oil rig that collects massive sensor data far away from the data center. The edge analytics lets the sensor data to access a decentralized platform and thereby performs analytics at the offshore and perhaps shuts down the flawed valves if any. This is considered as more efficient solution than sending data to data center or cloud environment and hang around for the same result much later [3].

Edge analytics provides following key benefits [4]:

- **Reduces Latency:** The decisions can be made faster and on time as the data is processed near to the source. This improves the liveliness and agility of an application.
- **Scalability:** As the number of network devices grows up, the quantity of data that is being collected and processed also rapidly increases. Edge analytics scales up the processing capabilities by providing the potential for decentralization.
- **Reduced Storage Costs:** The data is processed for necessary information prior to the storage. It reduces the storage cost as it is not necessary that all generated data are to be stored for many applications like autonomous vehicle, traffic management system, and so on.
- **Reduction of bandwidth:** The data to be transmitted to cloud are relatively reduced or filtered in the edge by processing it over there. Hence, it consumes comparatively low bandwidth.
- **Cost-effective:** The recovery will be usually faster even in distant locations as any failure that occurs in the analytics system can be predicted and avoided using data analytics mechanisms which prevents the loss that happens due to failure and reduces human interventions. Hence, edge analytics gives a cost-effective solution.
- **Preserves security and privacy:** Machine learning algorithms can be integrated to protect IoT from various attacks and to prevent unauthorized access.

3.9 POTENTIAL OF EDGE ANALYTICS

Though edge analytics is a blooming area, it might not be considered as a substitute for actual big data analytics. IoT along with the data analytics provides whole lot of advancements in various application domains. However, the biggest compromise of edge data analytics is that it analyses only the subset of data generated and transmits the analyzed results alone to the cloud. Remaining unprocessed data will be lost and never be stored at all. Hence, edge analytics is preferred only where this kind of data loss is negligible [7].

3.10 ARCHITECTURE OF EDGE ANALYTICS

Edge analytics is a method of enhancing IoT and cloud computing by analyzing data near to the source as shown in Fig. 3.9. Edge analytics aims at accessing computing resources in a more optimal way. Streaming and real-time data that are generated by IoT such as motor vehicles, home appliances, traffic lights, health care devices, and smart machineries can be processed at its point of source using localized edge server which can hold its own computing capability. In the meantime, intermediary servers can also be incorporated to the system to analyze data in proximity to the origin when needed. It reduces latency comparatively than the analytics done on the cloud infrastructure as the decision is made near to the data source. The time-sensitive decisions will not be made on time if the cloud servers does the analytics process. The quality of service is considerably increased in the edge analytics framework. Because the amount of data to be moved to cloud is reduced this in sequence minimizes the traffic and the transmission cost [3].

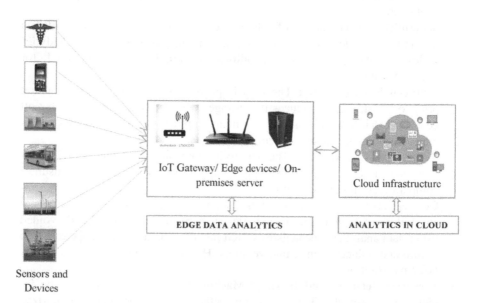

FIGURE 3.9 Architecture of edge analytics.

For instance, wind turbines use several electrical and optical sensors for variety of needs. Those sensors may help observe the vibration levels of wind turbine, temperature, the distance between other objects, and so on. The system need not send generated data persistently to the cloud analytics server. Instead, it can be designed to send data only when the data go beyond the threshold [1].

3.11   MACHINE LEARNING FOR EDGE DEVICES

TinyML is the field of study of machine algorithms that runs on less resource-intensive devices like mobile, microcontrollers, and other IoT devices. Inclusion of TinyML in smart IoT devices increases the latency as the data is processed on premises.

Tensor Flow Lite: Tensor Flow Lite is an open-source framework for making rapid inferences by means of Tensor Flow machine learning models on less resource-intensive devices such as mobile phones, IoT devices, and other embedded devices. It generates an optimized tiny model suitable for executing on common edge devices. The edge devices are less capable to handle huge dataset as it has limited processing power and memory. Inducing artificial intelligence to the devices leads to resource-intensive processes. Tensor Flow Lite is developed by considering these issues and it uses the workflow as shown in Fig. 3.10.

For the respective application, developing the custom deep learning model or pre-trained model is the foremost step at all times. Tensor Flow comes up with two additional components with the aim of transforming the current deep learning model to a lighter model which is capable to function on the target edge devices. Those components are Tensor Flow Lite Converter and Tensor Flow Lite Interpreter. Converter helps convert the custom Tensor Flow model to Tensor Flow Lite format. Interpreter helps to implement the Lite model to the target edge device by making use of various APIs. The model optimization can also be implemented so as to provide minimal changes in the performance of the model [10].

Federated Machine Learning: Machine learning model from different hosts can be integrated in order to preserve data privacy using federated learning approach. In many applications, data is residing at different places. Processing them altogether without disclosing the data to any central authority is the biggest challenge. In the applications like Image processing, combining different sources of data has become essential most of the times to provide adequate training and to build better model. Without centralized training data, federated learning unites the

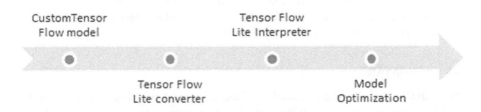

FIGURE 3.10   Working flow of Tensor Flow Lite framework.

models of various hosts. It addresses the issues related to privacy and security of the individual's data. It also helps edge data processing by keeping the data local instead of moving it to cloud. Federated machine learning ensures privacy-preserving data sharing among different entities without the involvement of cloud.

3.12   EDGE ANALYTICS: CASE STUDY

Corona Virus disease (COVID 19) is an infectious respiratory disease that had affected people all over the world. The only best way to safeguard ourselves is the social distancing. The organizations started deploying smart systems to keep track of these safety measure violations. The edge analytics-enabled smart CCTV systems significantly help in monitoring the people who move around the workplaces, malls, hospitals, universities, schools, restaurants, factories, and in all kinds of mass gatherings.

The key targets of the system are as follows:

- Helps monitor the total number of inhabitants in an environment
- Generate notifications to health and safety department in the organization to address the safety violations
- Facilitate well-programmed safety decisions

The working structure of this edge analytics-enabled CCTV system is as follows:

The CCTV videos are sent to IoT edge servers. The edge server constantly retrains the machine learning model. The model including object detection along with certain mathematical calculations is built to measure the distance among people to ensure the social distancing. The system alerts the respective personnel when the violation takes place [9].

3.13   RESEARCH CHALLENGES AND FUTURE RESEARCH DIRECTIONS

- Providing adequate security and privacy for the data when it is analyzed on premises is the key research field.
- While processing on the edge, only subset of data is analyzed. Missing out raw data might exclude some important insights.
- Approaches that facilitates to reduce the processing speed and processing power are the core objectives of implementing edge analytics. Improvements in the usage of those approaches are with developer's hands.
- IoT solutions are generally slow to make responses. Introducing the edge analytics may further reduce the latency.

3.14   SUMMARY

Data analytics is everywhere nowadays. Recent years have seen massive development in various domains with the gadget of new approaches using data analysis techniques. The IoT and cloud computing jointly functions as edge computing that is yet another thriving field in today's smart world. The data analytics doesn't fail to give its hold in edge computing as well. Dealing out streaming and massive data generated by smart IoT devices is the challenging task due to its size and processing time. Though, current approaches help process data in substantial delay, disseminating them to cloud storage is still a big challenge. Edge servers fixed either on premise or near to the data source are capable enough to do data analysis at the edge and it also helps to filter the data to be moved to the cloud. This in sequence builds a low latency, scalable, and cost-effective system. The analytics methods incorporated to smart systems yet again reduces the human interventions, automates the tasks and helps make decisions on time, and makes the smart systems to perform even smarter.

REFERENCES

1. Bonomi, F., Milito, R., Natarajan, P., & Zhu, J. (2014). Fog computing: A platform for internet of things and analytics. In: Bessis, N., and Dobre, C. (eds) *Big data and internet of things: A roadmap for smart environments*, Springer, Cham, 169–186
2. Marjani, M., Nasaruddin, F., Gani, A., Karim, A., Hashem, I. A., Siddiqa, A., & Yaqoob, I. (2017, March 29). Big IoT data analytics: Architecture, opportunities, and open research challenges. *IEEE Access*, 5, 5247–5261.
3. Azar, J., Makhoul, A., Barhamgi, M., & Couturier, R. (2019, July 1). An energy efficient IoT data compression approach for edge machine learning. *Future Generation Computer Systems*, 96, 168–175.
4. Naranjo, P. G., Pooranian, Z., Shojafar, M., Conti, M., & Buyya, R. (2019, October 1). FOCAN: A Fog-supported smart city network architecture for management of applications in the Internet of Everything environments. *Journal of Parallel and Distributed Computing*, 132, 274–283.
5. Huang, Y., Ma, X., Fan, X., Liu, J., & Gong, W. (2017, October 10). When deep learning meets edge computing. In *Proc. 2017 IEEE 25th International Conference on Network Protocols (ICNP)*, 1–2. IEEE.
6. Yassine, A., Singh, S., Hossain, M. S., & Muhammad, G. (2019, February 1). IoT big data analytics for smart homes with fog and cloud computing. *Future Generation Computer Systems*, 91, 563–573.
7. Patel, P., Ali, M. I., & Sheth, A. (2017, October 18). On using the intelligent edge for IoT analytics. *IEEE Intelligent Systems*, 32(5), 64–69.
8. Wang, X., Han, Y., Leung, V. C., Niyato, D., Yan, X., Chen, X. (2020, January 30). Convergence of edge computing and deep learning: A comprehensive survey. *IEEE Communications Surveys & Tutorials*, 22(2), 869–904.
9. Barthélemy, J., Verstaevel, N., Forehead, H., & Perez, P. (2019, January). Edge-computing video analytics for real-time traffic monitoring in a smart city. *Sensors*, 19(9), 2048.
10. Web Link: https://www.tensorflow.org/lite/guide

4 Edge Data Storage Security

4.1 DATA SECURITY

Deploying edge platforms without sacrificing security is indispensable as the edge devices are placed very close to the data and it is communicated to the central cloud server. Data security is at the forefront between edge and cloud communication and it acts as the key aspect of the framework. Data communication between edge and cloud is of three types:

- Very time-sensitive data
- Less time-sensitive data
- Data that are not time-sensitive

Very time-sensitive data is of response-oriented/analytics-oriented edge data. For any application, if the data need to be sent immediately for processing and taking decisions, it is categorized as very time-sensitive data. The objective is to minimize latency and to make spontaneous decisions/analyses for mission-critical applications such as oil rig/aircraft/missile launch. On the contrary, less time-sensitive data denotes the data that can wait for weeks. Data that are not time-sensitive are laid in the queue and, when it is required, sent to the central cloud server for processing/ analysis.

The core challenge involved is hardening the security system by safeguarding the data against intruders/attackers than abandoning. Security-based companies are tailoring security solutions abiding the regulations to meet the growing market demands to minimize the organization risks like disclosure, tampering, destruction, corruption, and theft. Many edge-based systems leverage conventional operating systems and host databases. Data confidentiality, integrity, secure data search, authentication, access control, and privacy-preserving are the wide spectrum of data security research architecture of edge computing as shown in Fig. 4.1. However, it is liable to attacks if classical cryptographic mechanisms are employed. To utilize the full spectrum of security measures, modern crypto mechanisms must be deployed. This chapter is limited to data confidentiality, authentication, and privacy-preserving approaches employed in edge computing. Under data confidentiality, the following schemes are likely to be discussed with its definition, illustration, working nature, and application [1].

- Homomorphic encryption
- Identity-based encryption (IBE)
- Attribute-based encryption

DOI: 10.1201/9781003230946-4

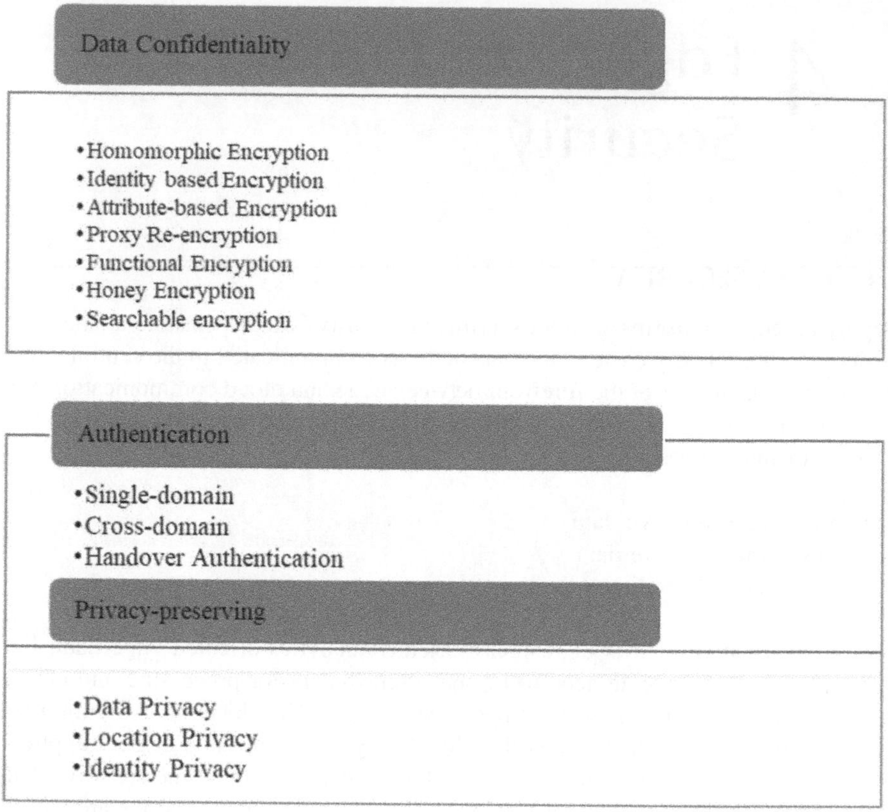

FIGURE 4.1 Data security research architecture.

- Proxy re-encryption
- Functional encryption
- Honey encryption
- Searchable encryption

With respect to authentication, the following schemes with its working principle will be discussed:

- Single-domain
- Cross-domain
- Handover authentication

In the topic of privacy-preserving, the given schemes are discussed with its nature of working.

- Data privacy
- Location privacy
- Identity privacy

4.2 DATA CONFIDENTIALITY

Manifold companies continue to combat invasive attacks against data. To manage and control the data theft/breaches in edge environment, appropriate data confidentiality schemes must be applied as the devices are data consumers and producers. These schemes must safeguard sensitive data using any encryption schemes. The conventional encryption schemes like AES/DES/RSA/ECC may be employed to the edge environment. However, accessing or processing ciphertext data for any analysis/query is quite low and makes it impossible to real adaptation. Manifold researches are carried out in recent years for secure data processing in edge framework. To assure confidentiality during outsourcing of data or processing the data either in edge/cloud, secure and reliable encryption techniques must be used. Efficient secure processing schemes are as follows:

    i. Identity-based encryption
    ii. Attribute-based encryption
    iii. Proxy re-encryption
    iv. Functional encryption
    v. Honey encryption
    vi. Searchable encryption
    vii. Homomorphic encryption

4.2.1 IDENTITY-BASED ENCRYPTION

Shamir [2] proposed an identity-based encryption scheme for certificate management initially. Any parties involved in the system can collaborate securely using this scheme by verifying one another's signatures without any negotiation of private/public keys. Public key infrastructure (PKI) or any third-party involvement is not essential for this scheme for its execution. Rather than using PKI, with this scheme, a key generator is used for generating the random number (seed). During encryption, when A sends mail to B, mail will be encrypted by the mail identifier of B and this acts as the public key for the transmission. On receiving the mail, B verifies himself/herself and receives a private key from the public key generator. With the aid of private key, mail will be decrypted as shown in Fig. 4.2.

To solve problems of identity in multi-party environment, enhanced IBE proposed [3] based on discrete logarithm problem that is considered to be NP-hard to strengthen the environment. Using bilinear maps, Boneh and Franklin [4] presented a scheme in 2003 using formal threshold cryptography.

4.2.2 ATTRIBUTE-BASED ENCRYPTION

It is a kind of encryption where secret key and ciphertext are based upon a set of attributes and thus intruders/attackers/outsiders are impossible to hold the ownership of the data. With the facilitation of trusted authority, attribute keys are published between the parties and used whenever necessary to decrypt. Decryption is based on the shared set of attributes after proper verification by trusted authority. It is primarily used for log encryption. Sahai and Waters [5] proposed a novel reuse sort of attribute-based encryption scheme. Key-based or ciphertext-policy-based attribute-based encryption is in use based on threshold value. Fig. 4.3 showcases the working of attribute-based encryption between the data owner and the users.

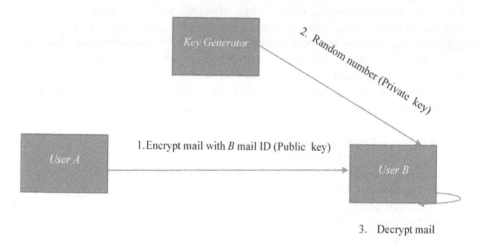

FIGURE 4.2   Identity-based encryption.

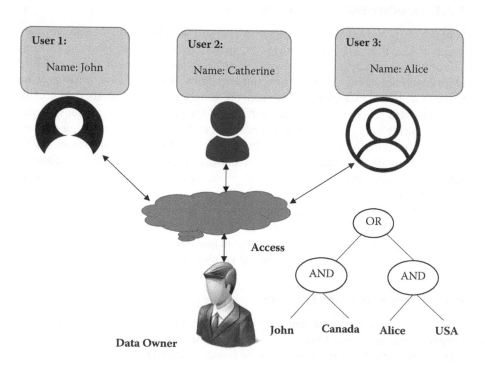

FIGURE 4.3   Attribute-based encryption.

4.2.3 PROXY RE-ENCRYPTION

Proxy re-encryption is a protocol devised by Blaze et al. [6], used to transform ciphertext of one key into ciphertexts for another with the help of a proxy. To put it in simple words, this method permits to convert a public key into another without having permission of ones' private key. This is possible using a key termed as re-encryption key and assures that the underlying original plaintext/message is not disclosed/altered. Due to this fascinating property, this is a widely adopted method in multi-user document/message sharing scenarios. Third-party is involved with this method to re-encrypt the message/document to send to other party.

Fig. 4.4 portrays the working principle of proxy re-encryption. Although this approach is proven to be strong under discrete logarithm problem that is of NP-hard, it still has few issues to be resolved. A major threat to this approach is, if proxy is an insider, there is a possibility to reverse process the information without the consent of user A or B. Similarly, both user A and proxy may act as insiders to process the information reversibly without the permission of user B. To resolve these issues, enhanced protocols were devised by many authors as their research work [1].

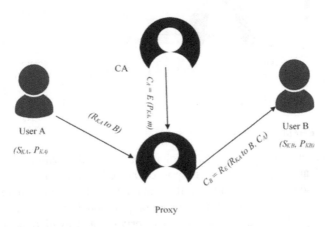

FIGURE 4.4   Proxy re-encryption.

4.2.4 FUNCTIONAL ENCRYPTION

A specific function is utilized with this approach to encrypt the data to send to other parties. Generally, it is a black-box function where the users can view the output without having any knowledge of the generated input. It enables the highest form of security and reliability to the edge environment. A lot of researches are ongoing in this area to design a robust function to avoid hazardous brute-force attacks. The security of this method depends on the function designed and it is a general form for attribute-based encryption and identity-based encryption. It was initially proposed by Amit et al. in 2005 and improved by Brent in 2010 [7]. In recent years, improvement is performed depth-wise on learning with errors assumption. Solving this approach is as hard as solving quantum-based problems.

4.2.5 HONEY ENCRYPTION

Honey encryption is a technique that is used to attract attackers/insiders by providing a captivating look, although it is a wrong plaintext obtained from decrypting the ciphertext. Honey encryption takes its root from one-time pad technique and the term "Honey" refers to fake/false resource. This technique is bounded with high probability and with a quite reasonable statistical model. It has been created for safeguarding the passwords against harmful brute-force attacks/breaches especially in web services related to financial transaction. It is closely related with format-preserving encryption (FPE) and format-transforming encryption (FTE) [8]. A simple representation of hone encryption is shown in Fig. 4.5.

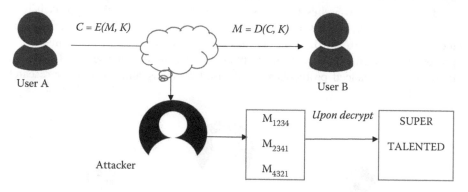

FIGURE 4.5   Honey encryption.

4.2.6 SEARCHABLE ENCRYPTION

Searching on encrypted data in an efficient manner is the primitive of searchable encryption. Searching and querying upon encrypted data receives recent attention toward the researchers' community that guarantees data confidentiality. This is considered an effective solution to reduce computational overhead for searching a word in encrypted database. It assures data privacy and availability to the collaborating parties. It is categorized as searchable symmetric encryption and searchable asymmetric encryption.

Fig. 4.6 shows the working nature of the searchable encryption scheme. Data in encrypted format are sent to the server. If the user/data owner intended to perform search operation upon the stored contents, based on the keyword search operation is performed and returned to the user with the help of trapdoor function. Trapdoor is a function used to retrieve the keywords that are linked with the users' secret key. It is a well-defined routine that does not reveal any information related to keywords. The security of these schemes relies on Discrete Diffie–Hellman (DDH) problem or Bilinear Diffie–Hellman (BDH) problem [9]. In searchable symmetric encryption, the same key is used for encryption, decryption, and trapdoor generation, whereas in searchable asymmetric encryption, different keys are employed. As a prerequisite, a bag of tags or keywords must be created to identify the message for a particular search.

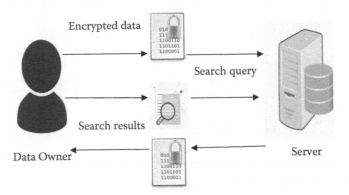

FIGURE 4.6 Searchable encryption.

4.2.7 HOMOMORPHIC ENCRYPTION

To enable operation on ciphertext directly with any number of arbitrary calculations, homomorphic encryption is formulated. It is well known as privacy homomorphism introduced by Rivest in 1978 that allows partial computations. In general, it converts data from one set to another by conserving the associations between them. The word "homomorphic" stands for "same structure". For instance, if we add two numbers in ciphertext and decrypt, the output must be equivalent to the output obtained by performing the same operation in plaintext. As the operations are carried out upon encrypted data, the computational overhead is reduced drastically and that is considered as the major benefit of homomorphic encryption. This guarantees transparency, efficient data processing, data retrieval, and secure data transmission with minimal timeframe even in an untrusted environment. It eliminates data breaches/attacks in a much wider sense. Most of the notable schemes represent the values as integers and use addition multiplication as the basic operations. The first plausible scheme was proposed by Craig Gentry in 2009 as an outcome of his Ph.D. dissertation. The thesis creates a new dimension for data processing and many researchers started to implement new schemes and few enhanced/optimized Gentry's scheme with formal proof of security [10]. Simple and secure homomorphic encryption schemes for healthcare applications are proposed by Anitha Kumari et al. [11] [16].

Common applications of homomorphic encryption are as follows:

- Secure data storage
- Data encryption
- Privacy-preserving
- Searching in encrypted data
- Secure data communication between multi-parties
- Supporting data analytics in encrypted data
- Querying data and retrieval

4.2.7.1 Types of Homomorphic Encryption

A general working of homomorphic encryption is given in Fig. 4.7. There exist three types of homomorphic encryption. The difference among the types is based on

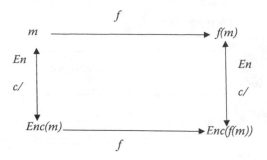

FIGURE 4.7   Working of homomorphic encryption.

the type and number of operations carried out in the ciphertext. The categories are as follows:

- Partially homomorphic encryption
- Somewhat homomorphic encryption
- Fully homomorphic encryption

Partially Homomorphic Encryption (PHE) and Somewhat Homomorphic Encryption (SHE)

Partially homomorphic encryption (PHE) supports one operative function, either addition or multiplication to get executed upon encrypted data unlimited number of times. Somewhat homomorphic encryption (SHE) supports addition or multiplication or both to execute limited number of times. RSA, ElGamal, Goldwasser–Micali, Paillier, and Boneh–Goh–Nissim are well-known PHE/SHE cryptosystems for decades. Fully homomorphic encryption (FHE) supports both the operations, addition and multiplication, to execute unlimited number of times. In this chapter, FHE is considered and substantiated.

Fully Homomorphic Encryption (FHE)

FHE allows unlimited number of operations with unlimited number of times. The circuit of FHE is predetermined and unbounded. This paves the way to explore more and receives attention from researchers in the current decade. It permits computation over encrypted data unlimitedly, both on-premises (edge device connected with smart devices) and off-premise data centers (cloud server). Several algorithms were designed and implemented to improve the accuracy and efficiency of FHE. Dijk et al. proposed an asymmetric encryption scheme based on computation over real integers by incorporating bootstrapping technique to reduce noise [12]. Another significant contribution in FHE is NTRU scheme [13]. In NTRU encryption scheme, arbitrary operations are based on the objects that are located in a truncated polynomial ring at the degree of N-1. A few recent works on FHE based on applications are listed as follows:

- An efficient algebraic homomorphic encryption scheme based on the Carmichael's theorem was proposed that works best for the integers. The scheme is used in applications such as electronic voting and multiparty computation. The operations involved in the Carmichael's encryption scheme are modular arithmetic in nature.

- A secured aerial photography using homomorphic encryption by considering the problem as the agents to encrypt the images and to upload it in the cloud server that is untrusted.
- Few HE schemes were proposed for the problems such as automated and real-time monitoring, automated bill processing, detection of energy loss, early warning of blackouts, fast detection of disturbances in energy supply, real-time energy planning, and pricing.
- Models like Cox Proportional Hazard Model and Logistic Regression Model are proposed for predictive analysis in health care. It is a standard way of encrypting data bitwise. The functions of these regression models are approximated by polynomial expressions in integer values. The advantage of this approach is that a single ciphertext carries numerous information than a single bit of plaintext. The limitation is that it restricts the possible operations to arithmetic circuits in the polynomials.
- An FHE embedding prototype to intrinsically ensure users' data confidentiality against threats in the working platform is a challenging application. The scheme comprises trans-ciphering, automatic compilation, parallelization, and message packing that allows performing homomorphic encryption in mere practice. This integrated platform is suitable for applications that are strongly dis-symmetric in nature and for applications that do not send any response back to the client device.
- An efficient hybrid homomorphic encryption technique for image encryption is presented to ensure the safe exchange of private images in the public cloud based on the block pixel position.

4.2.7.2 Basic Functions of Homomorphic Encryption

The security of most of the FHE is either based on Learning with Errors (LWE), Learning Parity with Noise (LPN), Learning with Rounding (LWR), or Ring-Learning with Errors (RLWE) problem, which is considered as NP-hard problem associated with lattices. Lattices are used to provide circuits with low multiplicative depth and intricacies that are proven to be secure against quantum attacks. The core functions of homomorphic encryption are as follows:

- Key generation
- Encryption
- Evaluation
- Decryption

The basic functions are elaborated in Fig. 4.8.

Any FHE supports two types of homomorphic schemes, namely, additive homomorphism and multiplicative homomorphism. A detailed view of additive and multiplicative homomorphisms is shown in Fig. 4.9.

Key generation: private key S_K; public key P_K

Encryption (Enc): $c = Enc\ (m,\ P_K)$; m - message

Decryption (Dec): $m = Dec(c,\ S_K)$

Evaluation (Eval): verify function whether $\psi \leftarrow Eval\ (P_K,$ $C,\ c_1,\ c_2....c_t) = Dec\ (S_K,\ \psi) = C\ (m_1,\ m_2....m_t)$; C - circuit

FIGURE 4.8   Basic functions of homomorphic encryption.

Additive Homomorphic Property:
$Enc_z(P_K, M_1) + Enc_z(P_K, M_2) = Enc_z(P_K, M_1 + M_2)$

Multiplicative Homomorphic Property:
$Enc_z(P_K, M_1) * Enc_z(P_K, M_2) = Enc_z(P_K, M_1 * M_2)$

FIGURE 4.9   Additive and multiplicative homomorphic properties.

Few of the schemes listed under data confidentiality are still in elusive stage and it is a completely open platform for improvement and application in edge computing environment.

4.3 AUTHENTICATION

Proper authentication mechanisms are mandate for any federated environment, failing leads to access by outsiders/adversaries. Verification of ones' own identity with the credentials is referred to as authentication. Most of the edge environment mandates identity validation in trusted domains. The most suitable authentication mechanisms for edge computing environment are listed as follows:

- Single-domain authentication
- Cross-domain authentication
- Handover authentication

4.3.1 SINGLE-DOMAIN AUTHENTICATION

Authentication must ensure verification, data anonymity, user privacy, and forward security. Data anonymity says any illegitimate user must not gain access to the communication even if the communication occurs in an open public channel. User privacy must not be tampered unless or otherwise the users already agreed for mutual concern/interest. Forward security guarantees that none of the previous messages exchanged is disclosed to the interceptors. Manifold researches are on-going in this area to harden the security and to preserve the privacy. Anonymous

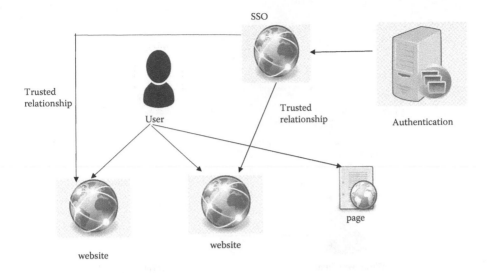

FIGURE 4.10   Single-domain authentication.

authentication and privacy-preserving are assured in the system model proposed by Liu et al. [14] with high level of scalability. Privacy-aware authentication scheme proposed by Jiang et al. [15] provides single-domain-based authentication using bilinear pairing cryptosystem and dynamic nonce generation. This scheme offers mutual authentication by mitigating all possible threats in large-scale distributed environment. An enhanced version of this scheme is presented by including identity-based signatures. Much simplest way of single-domain authentication is Single Sign-On (SSO). Once SSO is set up, the users with proper verification could be able to access all the services provided by the company within the premises. SSO empowers users to access manifold services/applications/websites by logging in only once. For instance, managing Google Accounts with SSO support irrespective of the devices is a captivating feature to access all the facilities in a single layout after logging in only once. A seamless, safe, and secure environment is provided to the consumers using OAuth 2.0 protocol. Fig. 4.10 illustrates the working of single-domain authentication.

4.3.2   Cross-Domain Authentication

When the request for user authentication is made across domain, it is referred to as cross-domain authentication. For instance, if the requests from one application along with credentials are sent to another domain that differs from the current application domain for its service, it is called cross-domain authentication. Gathering the requested users' credentials from an application and sending them to another origin obviously encounters security threats/vulnerabilities/breaches. To alleviate these attacks, proper security controls/measures must be taken and deployed to ensure guaranteed access across the domains. This can be achieved through attribute-based framework or group key policy-based framework.

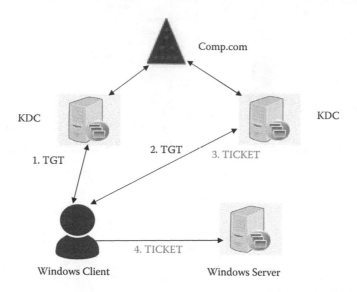

FIGURE 4.11 Cross-domain authentication.

Hierarchical tree-based structure and high level of scalability maintenance is mandated for group key policy-based framework, whereas attribute-based authentication framework is considered as the next-generation model as it is context-aware and offers dynamic access control. Although many schemes exist in these models, key/certificate revocation, privacy-preserving, and anonymous authentication are considered as the major limitation of these schemes and paves way for improvement. Fig. 4.11 details the cross-domain authentication that exists between two company entities.

4.3.3 HANDOVER AUTHENTICATION

To ensure secure and seamless roaming over multiple access points of the wireless devices, proper mandate authentication is indispensable and is termed as handover authentication. Designing an efficient handover authentication protocol is considered to be a cumbersome process as it is liable to very frequent hazardous attacks. In addition, scalability and processing overhead are considered the highest limitations of handover authentication. Untraceability and identity privacy must be the primitive properties to be satisfied by this technique. Many such schemes exist by preserving anonymous authentication using classical hard cryptosystems such as ElGamal and elliptic curve cryptography. A typical handover authentication scenario is portrayed in Fig. 4.12.

4.4 PRIVACY-PRESERVING SCHEMES

Ensuring privacy in the edge computing environment is an unavoidable task. The environment must assure holistic privacy, conditional privacy, trajectory privacy,

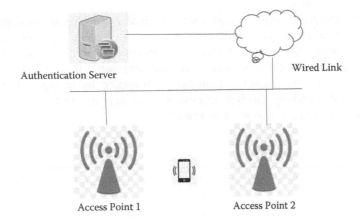

FIGURE 4.12 Handover authentication.

differential privacy, data privacy, location privacy, and identity privacy. Out of these privacies, data privacy, location privacy, and identity privacy are the mandate privacy policies to get executed. To enforce the highest level of security, fine-grained privacy policy execution is extremely important.

4.4.1 DATA PRIVACY

A humongous amount of data is generated every day from various applications/ sectors, such as e-commerce, retail, social media, banks, and so on, due to un-precedented digital transformation. Apparently, this paves the way to serious/ harmful privacy violations. Key threats considered are as follows:

- Disclosure
- Discrimination
- Surveillance
- Individual data abuse

Data privacy, also referred to as information privacy, is used to protect the privacy of data such that illegal user must not own data access. Proper mechanisms of reasonable importance must be adopted for collecting, sharing, and using the data, especially when dealing with personal data. Any sector must have the responsibility in providing:

- Proper consent in collection data especially individuals
- Assurance of data quality
- Lucid statement/agreement for data collection
- Purpose for data collection
- Assurance for data protection
- Transparency in policies and procedures
- Accountability statement

Various privacy-preserving techniques were devised and deployed to safeguard the personal data abiding the regulations such as K-anonymity, L-diversity, T-closeness, randomization, and cryptographic techniques. Probabilistic public-key encryption is considered as one of the technical approaches that preserves the data privacy efficiently. An improvised method is proposed by incorporating ranked keyword-based searching. Such a scheme is more appropriate to edge-cloud environment by providing high level of scalability.

4.4.2 LOCATION PRIVACY

Location privacy is the individual's right to decide when and for what purposes the information can share with others. Maintaining the privacy preservation of location of the users is a rudimentary process in edge environment. If proper measures are not taken, adversaries perform various attacks, such as

- User profiling
- Political/religious discrimination
- Denial of service
- Physical attacks
- Illegal advertisement

Constructing a secure positioning protocol with location privacy in the bounded retrieval mode is one of the finest options to preserve the location privacy. Several approaches exist and preserve location privacy via dummy location updates, distributed cache proxy servers, creating fake locations to the attackers, obfuscation-based techniques by ensuring high level of scalability.

4.4.3 IDENTITY PRIVACY

Identity/users privacy is the one that safeguards the user's privacy without sacrificing the quality. It is one of the highest challenges one must take care of as many businesses are grooming to track end consumers' behavior and to market it. In recent times, mushroom of brokering agents used to consolidate and sell personal information of individuals to the competing companies/government agencies. The best way to maintain identity privacy is by limit profiling. Dynamic credential generation, cross-domain trusted third-party managerial authentication is considered as the best possible approach to maintain identity privacy of the users. Most of the protocols support ad hoc mobile environment and recent researches are stepped into fog-mobile computing environment.

4.5 EDGE-BASED ATTACK DETECTION AND PREVENTION

Major attack-based challenges involved in edge computing are privacy leakage, denial of service attacks, unauthorized access by adversaries and data tampering. To process the massive data efficiently by satisfying confidentiality and privacy properties and to provide mutual authentication, traditional schemes are no longer suitable. External or internal adversaries on gaining access may abuse the privileges assigned. Unauthorized access can be eliminated by applying novel authentication mechanisms like cross-domain authentication and hand-over authentication. By deploying servers at the edge of the network, conventional denial of service and its associated attacks can be prevented. Another highest challenge is the data tampering and physical assaults on edge infrastructure. Stringent physical protection must be provided for the edge infrastructure and to evade data tampering modern confidentiality schemes with its core benefits are discussed in Section 4.2. For safe and secure conversion of one's public key into another, proxy based a third-party access method, namely, proxy re-encryption is in practice. Similarly to send and receive messages securely in multi-party environment, attribute-based encryption is preferred. All false/bogus accessing of resources and harmful brute force attacks/breaches can be avoided using honey encryption. In addition, homomorphic encryption is used to avoid data breaches and invasive attacks in edge environment by performing all kinds of operations upon encrypted data rather than on plain text. Privacy leakage is considered another key threat in edge system. To detect privacy leakage complete surveillance must be maintained and robust modern privacy-preserving mechanisms must be adopted alike located based privacy scheme. Thus, by applying the above-discussed methods in edge computing systems multi-source data processing is performed in a safe and secure manner without compromising the transmission speed. It also provides rich user experience and mobility support.

4.6 CONCLUSION AND FUTURE RESEARCH DIRECTIONS

In this chapter, edge computing data storage systems are discussed in detail with figures and illustrations wherever necessary. Contemporary data confidentiality schemes working principle, challenges, and its countermeasures are elaborated for a holistic edge computing environment. Definition of homomorphic encryption, functions, properties and its applications are analyzed and presented in detail for the upcoming researchers. The later part analyzes the modern authentication mechanisms and privacy-preserving schemes for solving verification and privacy issues in edge framework. Open research areas of data security and privacy in edge computing is detailed in Section 4.5. Future research may shed light on devising distributed lightweight authentication and encryption schemes that are more suitable to edge systems. Another highest challenge in existing privacy-preserving schemes is the dynamic update functionality. Searching speed and accuracy can be enhanced in multi-party, multi-user in different trust domains. During offloading process, a verifiable computing procedure may be adopted to increase the computational accuracy.

REFERENCES

1. Zhang, J., Chen, B, Zhao, Y, Cheng, X, & Hu, F. (2018). Data security and privacy-preserving in edge computing paradigm: Survey and open issues. *IEEE Access*, *26*, 18209–18237.

2. Shamir, A. (1984). Identity-based cryptosystems and signature schemes. In *Advances in cryptology (Lecture Notes in Computer Science)* (Vol. 196, 47–53). Santa Barbara, CA: Springer.

3. Tsujii, S., & Itoh, T. (1989). An ID-based cryptosystem based on the discrete logarithm problem. *IEEE Journal on Selected Areas in Communications, 7*(4), 467–473.

4. Boneh, D., & Franklin, M. (2003). Identity-based encryption from the Weil pairing. *SIAM Journal on Computing, 32*(3), 586–615.

5. Sahai, A., & Waters, B. (2005, May). Fuzzy identity-based encryption. In *Proc.*, Aarhus, Denmark, 457–473.

6. Blaze, M., Bleumer, G., & Strauss, M. (1998, May). Divertible protocols and atomic proxy cryptography. In *Proc. 17th International Conference on the Theory and Applications of Cryptographic Techniques.*, Espoo, Finland, 127–144.

7. Boneh, D., Sahai, A., & Waters, B. (2012). Functional encryption: A new vision for public-key cryptography. *ACM Communications, 55*(11), 56–64.

8. Yin, W., Indulska, J., & Zhou, H. (2017). Protecting private data by honey encryption. *Security and Communication Networks, 2017*, 1–9.

9. Boneh, D., & Waters, B. (2007). Conjunctive, subset, and range queries on encrypted data. In *Theory of cryptography* (Vol. 4392, 535–554). Amsterdam, Netherlands: Springer.

10. Gentry, C., & Halevi, S. (2011). Implementing gentry's fully homomorphic encryption scheme. In *Proc. Annual International Conference on the Theory and Applications of Cryptographic Techniques (EUROCRYPT 2011)*, 129–148.

11. Anitha Kumari, K., Sharma, A., Chakraborty, C., & Ananyaa, M. (2021). Preserving Health Care Data Security and Privacy Using Carmichael's Theorem-Based Homomorphic Encryption and Modified Enhanced Homomorphic Encryption Schemes in Edge Computing Systems. *BigData*. Mary Ann Liebert Publishers Ahead of Print. DoI: https://doi.org/10.1089/big.2021.0012.

12. Dijk, M., Gentry, C., Halevi, S., & Vaikuntanathan, V. (2010). Fully homomorphic encryption over the integers. In *Proc. Annual International Conference on the Theory and Applications of Cryptographic Techniques (EUROCRYPT 2010)*, 24–43

13. Liu, B., & Wu, H. (2016). Efficient multiplication architecture over truncated polynomial ring for NTRUEncrypt system. In *Proc. IEEE Conferences in International Symposium on Circuits and Systems (ISCAS)*, 1174–1177.

14. Liu, H., Ning, H., Xiong, Q., & Yang, L. T. (2015). Shared authority based privacy-preserving authentication protocol in cloud computing. *IEEE Transactions on Parallel and Distributed Systems, 26*(1), 241–251.

15. Jiang, Q., Ma, J., & Wei, F. (2018). On the security of a privacy-aware authentication scheme for distributed mobile cloud computing services. *IEEE Systems Journal, 12*(2), 2039–2042.

16. Kumari, K. A., Indusha, M., & Dharani, D. (2021). Enhanced Human Activity Recognition based on Activity Tracker Data Using Secure Homomorphic Encryption Techniques. *In Proc. 2nd International Conference for Emerging Technology (INCET)*, 1–7.

5 Blockchain and Edge Computing Systems

5.1 HISTORY OF BLOCKCHAIN

In the year 2008, Satoshi Nakamoto invented a trustless digital currency called Bitcoin (BTC) in order to eliminate the third-party mediators in digital financial transactions. In the concept of Bitcoin, the transactions in a peer-to-peer (P2P) network are verified using cryptographic mechanism and the transaction records are stored in the distributed ledger. Here, the successful mining process will be rewarded with bitcoins. Bitcoin mining is a practice of releasing bitcoins for circulation. In order to add a block in blockchain, miner requires solving a computationally strong puzzle to get a reward in terms of bitcoins. This Bitcoin is the first application that uses blockchain technology. In the year 2009, with 50 bitcoins of rewards, Nakamoto mined the first block of bitcoins called the genesis block. The first Bitcoin transaction was done by Hal Finney who had downloaded Bitcoin software and obtained ten bitcoins from Nakamoto. Bitcoin was released as opensource software that facilitated many cryptocurrency developers to design different cryptocurrencies that mimic bitcoins. Satoshi is the person who initiated the usage of consensus mechanisms. The Bitcoin network provides evidence that Proof of Work (PoW) consensus is an approach that effectively validates and verifies peers in the Bitcoin network. Till the year 2014, Bitcoin was used merely as the cryptocurrency. In 2014, Vitalik Buterin planned to take advantage of Bitcoin for other domains and purposes apart from cryptocurrency. Subsequently, he introduced smart contracts and tried integrating to Bitcoin network. Upon the opposition by the Bitcoin organization, he developed his own blockchain called Ethereum with its own cryptocurrency called ether (ETH). In the second generation of blockchain, it integrated business logic in the form of smart contracts to the applications along with the cryptocurrencies. At present, the ETH is the second-largest cryptocurrency in the world subsequent to BTC. In the year 2015, Linux Foundation along with IBM, Intel, and SAP Ariba developed a private blockchain for enterprise organizations called Hyperledger. As a result, speed of the transactions was increased and highly scalable such that small blockchain networks were designed to meet the expectations of individual organizations. This was the third generation in the evolution of blockchain network [1].

5.2 DISTRIBUTED LEDGER TECHNOLOGY

In the traditional document sharing system, the multiple authorities cannot pool resources where the information cannot be simultaneously managed or processed. For instance, if person A updates and sends a document to person B, altogether

DOI: 10.1201/9781003230946-5

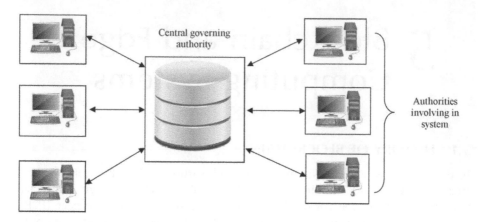

FIGURE 5.1 Centralized system.

person B cannot update or modify it. He/she has to update the most recent document and resend it to person A again which is a time-consuming process even for a minor update. Then, the introduction to centralized platforms had resolved this kind of issue partially by appointing a central authority/medium to maintain the document where the updation is done simultaneously as shown in Fig. 5.1. At the same time, as the complete reliance on the single node is not secure, the centralized document sharing mechanism came up with a single point of failure problem.

Decentralized storage mechanism is a feasible solution that provides authority to multiple local authorities rather than a single node. Decentralized organizations rely on local community, thus eliminates single point of failure as shown in Fig. 5.2. Multiple points of coordination are required in decentralized system. Hence, the failure of any local governing authority may result in disconnected networks [2].

Distributed networks are groups of nodes where every node is independent and interconnected to each other. Blockchain is a distributed and immutable database that functions without the involvement of any central monitoring authority. Data are not stored in a centralized place which prevents it from being lost. Hence, every individual entity in the network is equally privileged. Every individual node in a network maintains a local copy of the global data sheet. It is called as distributed ledger that maintains all transactions among entities of a network with time stamp so as to maintain tamper-resistant data as shown in Fig. 5.3. There are two types of ledger models that are currently in use by various blockchain frameworks. Unspent Transaction Output (UTXO) model is used by the Bitcoin network. Account balance model is used in Hyperledger and Ethereum blockchain frameworks.

The distributed database distributes the content/data in different systems which are controlled and monitored by single entity. The blockchain distributed architecture is a network in which every node acts as an administrator. Each transaction in network is cryptographically verified and validated before it is being added to distributed ledger. Once a transaction is updated in blockchain, it is impossible to modify it. The ledger is comparable to the Linked List data structure as it is a cryptographically linked chain of blocks. Each of these blocks contains transactions

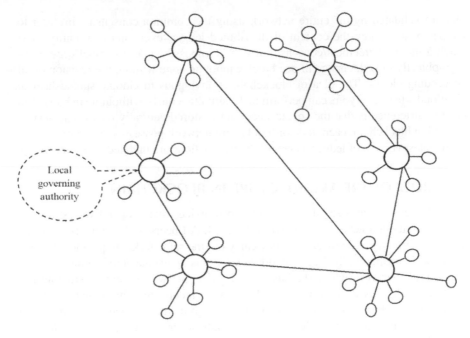

FIGURE 5.2 Decentralized system.

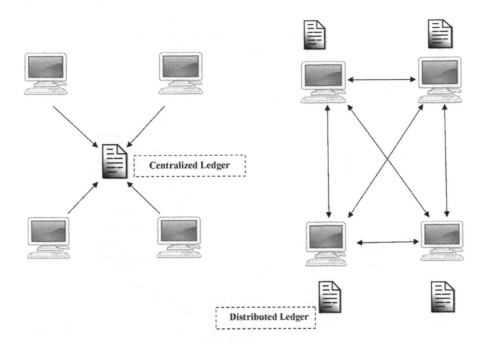

FIGURE 5.3 Centralized vs. distributed ledger.

that are validated by the entire network using the common consensus. In order to tamper or to change the content of distributed ledger, every network entity must reach a mutual agreement/consensus which is impossible. As the blocks are cryptographically linked, change in one block cannot be done without the revision of all succeeding blocks. The idea of blockchain is analogous to Google spreadsheet in the cloud where everyone can perform tasks simultaneously without losing any data but the difference is that the spreadsheet data is stored centrally on Google server. Instead in blockchain, each node of blockchain network possesses an identical copy of the latest version of ledger where all the transactions are updated with timestamp.

5.3   ROLE OF P2P ARCHITECTURE IN BLOCKCHAIN

The P2P network consists of a group of peers/devices that cooperatively store and share the data in a network as shown in Fig. 5.4. All peers in the network have the identical authority and power, and they carry out the same tasks. In payment service networks like Bitcoin, the P2P network generally is an exchange of digital assets in a distributed network where the buyers and sellers act without any intermediaries.

Blockchain integrates the idea of P2P network architecture and maintains a distributed ledger which every actor can trust, although the actors themselves might not be familiar with each other. The cryptographically secured P2P network architecture with Distributed Ledger Technology (DLT) prevents the problem of double spending possible in digital asset transactions. Double spending is the process of spending the same money to more than one entity where with physical money/cash systems it is impractical. A blockchain system combines cryptography solutions, P2P network features, and game theory aspects. Usage of public key cryptography and cryptographic hash functions ensures the transparency and privacy of transactions happening

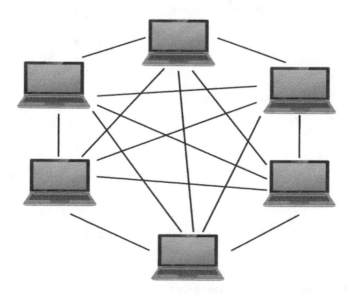

FIGURE 5.4   P2P network.

in the network. Blockchain network is managed by decentralized community over a P2P network through incentivization. Generally, game theory is a study of deliberate decision-making process. Here the transactions are validated using consensus mechanisms and the node that won in the validation process adds the next block to the chain and also the node gets economic incentives. The miner of the network whoever running the consensus algorithm and adding the block to the blockchain is given incentives. This process is called minting. The process of adding the next block to the blockchain based on consensus mechanism reminds the properties of game theory [3].

5.4 BLOCKCHAIN CRYPTOGRAPHY

Cryptographic techniques are used in blockchain to ensure confidentiality, authenticity, authorization, non-repudiation, and integrity. Confidentiality in a transaction refers to the responsibility to guarantee that the information shared is kept secret. It is the ability to convert a readable message into unreadable format so as to improve privacy. Authenticity is the process of confirming the user's identity to proceed further transactions. Authorization is the process of providing user permission to access a specific resource. Non-repudiation proves whether the sender really sent this message or not. Integrity makes sure that the message is not tampered during the transmission as shown in Fig. 5.5 [4].

Blockchain technology uses cryptography mechanisms in multiple ways: for instance, for wallets, transactions, security, and privacy preservation. The following are the most extensively used cryptographic techniques in blockchain:

- Public key cryptography
- Hashing
- Merkle tree
- Digital signature

Public Key Cryptography (Asymmetric Key Cryptography): In symmetric key mechanisms, a single secret key is used for both encryption and decryption processes. Although these systems are fast and efficient, a separate key is required for every user. For N users in a system, $N*(N-1)/2$ keys are needed. Storing and maintaining these large numbers of key secure and transmitting the key among parties is an issue. Hence, blockchain uses public key cryptography mechanisms.

Asymmetric key cryptography uses two keys: private key and public key. If person A wants to transfer a message to person B, person A encrypts the message using person B's public key which is available to everyone in public. Person A transmits an encrypted message to person B. Person B then decrypts the message using its own private key which is not present to anybody else. Here, public key is derived from private key but vice versa is impossible.

Commonly used public key cryptography technique is RSA. In blockchain, even more secure and faster public key cryptographic mechanism called elliptic curve cryptography (ECC) is used. With key of size 256 bits, ECC achieves more security compared to key of size 3072 bits in RSA [5]. ECC algorithm provides better security with smaller key size than RSA. ECC is based on non-singular elliptic

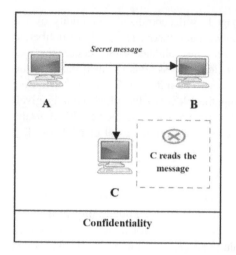

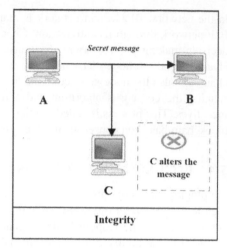

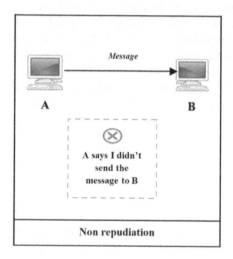

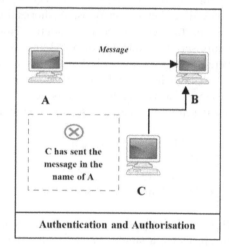

FIGURE 5.5 Cryptographic properties.

curves and points arithmetic concepts, hence it is secure and faster. The following is an elliptic curve equation:

$$y^2 = x^3 + ax + b$$

Consider M is the message to be transmitted. Public key (Q) is derived using private key d in range 1 to N-1. For instance, public key is generated using the formula Q = d * P, where P is a point in the elliptic curve, d is private key, and Q is public key.

ECC Encryption: Randomly select k from 1 to N-1. "m" is message to be transferred and represented by M on the elliptic curve. Hence, two ciphertexts C1 and C2 are generated using point arithmetic techniques as below.

$$C1 = k * P$$

$$C2 = M + k * Q$$

ECC Decryption: Original message (M) is extracted from two ciphertexts C1 and C2 using private key (d) as below.

$$M = C2 - d * C1$$

Hashing: Hashing is a process of transforming the text of arbitrary length to a text of fixed length. The main objective of hashing is to preserve integrity. Bitcoin network uses SHA-256 as hashing mechanism. Keccak is a modified version of SHA and it is used in Ethereum blockchain network which is faster than SHA. A strong hashing algorithm must satisfy the following properties:

- Even a small change in the input data produces a drastic difference in the output. It is called as avalanche effect.
- Hashing is always one-way function and it ensures that the original text cannot be retrieved back. Given H(x), it must be computationally difficult to find x.
- It must be collision free. This property ensures the unique hash value.

Hashing can either be linear hash or tree-based hash. Since the transactions are dynamic, linear hashing is not suitable for blockchain. Rehashing is required for every insertion and it must traverse all the nodes every time. Hence, tree-based hash is used in blockchain. In this regard, rehashing is needed only when the specific path has to be recomputed. It reduces the complexity to log N.

Merkle Hash Tree: Every transaction in blockchain is hashed using algorithms like SHA-256 and maintained in a data structure called Merkle tree in blockchain. The leaf nodes are the hash values of valid transactions, respectively. The intermediate nodes are generated by rehashing the hash values of leaf nodes. This process continues till root node. Each and every node in the Merkle tree is interlinked using hash value which makes it computationally strong and secure. Merkle root is then added to block header to integrate the pool of valid transactions to corresponding block in the blockchain. This data structure is extensively used in Bitcoin and Ethereum blockchain networks.

Digital Signature: To ensure authentication, integrity, and non-repudiation, the digital signature is integrated in blockchain. The sender first hashes the transaction/message data using a hash function (double SHA-256 is used in Bitcoin) for later verification of data integrity. The hashed data are then encrypted using the sender's private key to provide authentication and the encrypted output is known as the digital signature of that transaction. The encrypted message digest is called the digital signature. The transaction data and the digital signature are broadcasted to network. At the receiver end, the digital signature is decrypted using public key of the sender to obtain message digest. Message digest is

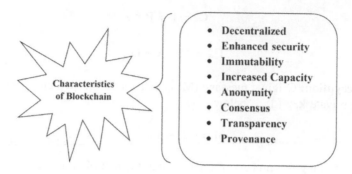

FIGURE 5.6 Characteristics of blockchain.

again calculated separately from the received data. This is checked to notice if it is the same as message digest decrypted from the digital signature. Hence, the digital signature can be used to provide authentication, ensuring integrity and non-repudiation. Elliptic Curve Digital Signature Algorithm (ECDSA) is widely used in blockchain for providing digital signature and it uses ECC to create key pairs that are used for signing and verification process [4].

5.5 CHARACTERISTICS OF BLOCKCHAIN

The basic characteristics of blockchain are as follows (Fig. 5.6):

Decentralized: No single authority can control the blockchain network. It is a P2P decentralized distributed ledger.

Enhanced Security: Blockchain integrates the cryptographic techniques such as digital signature, public key cryptography, and hashing mechanisms to maintain integrity. Blockchain network is verifiable. Whenever a block initiates a transition, other network entities verify and validate whether the transition is correct or not. If the data are tampered, the cryptographic signature will become invalid and hence it cannot be verified and validated by network entities.

Immutability: The immutability in blockchain is achieved through the ledger. Once the blocks are added to blockchain, it cannot be modified as it is crypto-graphically more secure and minor changes in data cause a huge difference in the generated hash. Blockchain is growing list of records called blocks. Every generated block in blockchain is linked to previous block using its hash value. Change in any one block affects all the successive blocks. Cryptographically altering all the further blocks is impossible.

Increased Capacity: As there are many nodes/computers working together, blockchain offers greater power than the centralized system.

Anonymity: In blockchain, the account numbers of individuals are public but it does not expose the private, identity details such as name of the person involved in the transaction. From the account number, other personal details of the individuals cannot be fetched as the account numbers are exposed only after hashed.

Consensus: Each network participant keeps a copy of the entire blockchain. Consensus validates and verifies every new transaction. It is generally validated by network miners who are incentivized to verify transactions through consensus mechanisms like PoW. As there is no central controlling authority in blockchain network, each and every node works independently. Consensus is intended to ensure consistency of transactions between nodes without anomalies.

Transparency: Everyone who joined in network can view the public accounts and it's all the transactions but private information of public accounts are not exposed to the network entities.

Provenance: In order to establish trust and authenticity, the history of the transactions is recorded in blocks of a blockchain. Origin of the transactions can easily be tracked and monitored. Anyone who transacts in network can be traced and this feature helps trace the provenance of a network entity.

5.6 BENEFITS AND LIMITATIONS OF BLOCKCHAIN

BENEFITS

- Nobody has the central authority. Human involvement in the verification and validation process improves trust and accuracy.
- Modifying the assets is practically impossible as the degree of decentralization makes it complicated to alter.
- All the activities that happen in network are open to every other network entity to observe. This property provides a transparency in the network, meanwhile it ensures the transactions are secured, private, and efficient.
- Though blockchain is slow depending on the network congestion, it eradicates the excessive cost to be spent for transaction as it eliminates third-party verification.
- It is well suited for a network where users don't trust each other.

LIMITATIONS

- The PoW consensus in Bitcoin takes around 10 minutes to add a block into the chain. Solution for this concern is under research for years. Speed ineffectiveness is the major concern with the blockchain network.
- It takes high computational power to validate each transaction. Though it eliminates third-party verification costs, the electricity consumption for validating blocks becomes the most important concern.

5.7 TYPES OF BLOCKCHAIN

There are two primary types in blockchain, namely, private blockchain and public blockchain. Later, different variations of blockchain have arrived. Irrespective of the types, blockchain network has the following common properties:

- It is a P2P network.
- The transactions are updated in distributed ledger.

- Every node in a blockchain network has a copy of shared and distributed ledger.
- Each node validates and verifies the transactions that take place in network through consensus and various cryptographic mechanisms.

Degree of Centralization is a key attribute based on which the categorization of the blockchain is determined. The most important threats in totally centralized system are the trust among the entities and single point of failure. Decentralization and various metrics in blockchain help establish trust among parties and avoid single point of failure. Blockchain configuration varies across different categories as shown in Fig. 5.7.

Private Blockchain: Private blockchain restricts the actors joining the network as it is permissioned network. It preserves privacy. The network is more energy efficient compared with public blockchain as it has its own private consensus mechanisms that work faster. These are less volatile networks. It is well suited for any particular organization. Transaction throughput is higher than public blockchain. All the members who are present in the network are authenticated or pre-approved to join in. So, less energy-intensive consensus algorithms like simple voting mechanisms is also preferred here. Private Blockchain is also referred to as partially decentralized network since it is controlled by organization to some extent. A simple and secure blockchain for Internet of Medical Things (IoMT) using private blockchain is illustrated by Anitha Kumari et al. [6].

Public Blockchain: In public blockchain networks, any people can join without authentication and participate in the consensus. Privacy is less and it consumes more energy to run the consensus. Public blockchains are volatile networks since any participant can join or leave the network as per their wish. This type of network

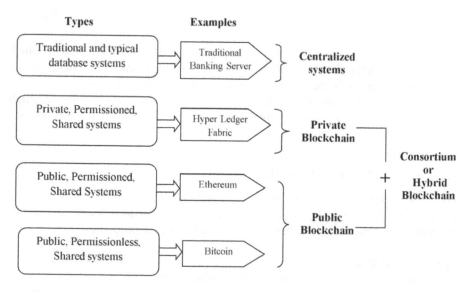

FIGURE 5.7 Types of blockchain.

is fully decentralized and transparent. An example of fully transparent, permissionless, decentralized public blockchain is Bitcoin network. Public blockchain can also be of permissioned networks. In that regard, the network entities are validated before joining the network. An example of permissioned public blockchain is Ethereum blockchain. Public blockchain makes use of native assets or currencies. For instance, Ethereum uses ethers as its currency. Bitcoin network uses Bitcoin currency as its rewards. Private blockchain does not bother much about the currencies.

Consortium/Hybrid Blockchain: Consortium/hybrid network is a mixture of public and private blockchain. It integrates the advantages of both the network types such as volatility, authentication, privacy, and immutability. It also reduces energy cost. It balances between the two types. Though membership in hybrid blockchain is private, it is public in governance perspective. It is much more energy-efficient and has privacy than permissionless network. An example of consortium blockchain is Ethermint [7].

5.8 BLOCKCHAIN ARCHITECTURE AND FUNDAMENTALS

Bitcoin is the first network that introduced blockchain technology. The transactions in a Bitcoin P2P network happen as shown in Figs. 5.8 and 5.9. For any node to participate in the blockchain transactions, it must have a wallet. It is a program that is used for interacting in the blockchain network. A typical blockchain wallet contains private key of the user. It examines incoming and outgoing cryptocurrency

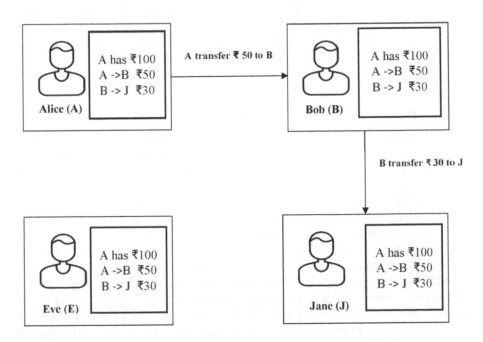

FIGURE 5.8   Transaction in blockchain.

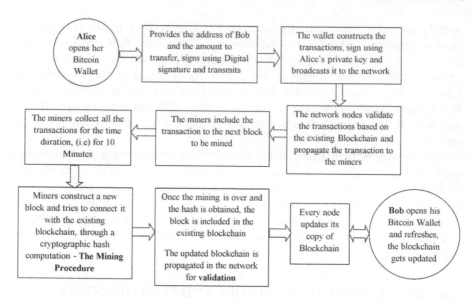

FIGURE 5.9 Transaction workflow.

to the account. For sending cryptocurrency to other account, digital signature is formed with the help of the private key present in the wallet and the same is verified on the other side using public key. A wallet in a blockchain is similar to that of the account passbook given for a user of a bank that is unique for an account. Cryptocurrency operates on top of blockchain and is described as virtual money. It is also decentralized and cryptographically secured which no single authority can control and monitor like blockchain network. A blockchain network can function with or without cryptocurrency depending on the type of the blockchain. Typically private blockchain does not focus on cryptocurrency or token-based systems.

5.8.1 BLOCKCHAIN BEHIND BITCOIN NETWORK

In blockchain, all the nodes in a network maintain a consistent copy of distributed ledger. Every participant in the network is called node. Nodes in the blockchain network can be categorized into three distinct types: light node, full node, and mining node.

Light Node: Light node is also called simple node that does not hold the complete transaction details. It holds the wallet information such as account number and private key of individual user, and initiates new transaction in a network. Since it is not holding the ledger, light-weight nodes are not a part of blockchain network. So this type of nodes does not participate in validating other transactions.

Full Node: Full nodes are also called validators and these are the part of blockchain network. It holds the complete transaction history in the form of shared ledger. The ledgers in every full node of a blockchain hold consistent information. It is not responsible to propose a new block but it can initiate the transaction and maintain wallet information. The major responsibility of the full node is to validate every transaction. Validation is to ensure whether the wallet has adequate amount to complete the transaction and also verifies the credibility of the entities through its digital signature. In Fig. 5.8, all the nodes (A), (B), (J), and (E) are examples of full nodes as all hold the shared ledger in Bitcoin network.

Mining Node: Mining node is a full node and contains mining function. It is also called block generator. These are the actors or computers responsible to propose a new block by solving cryptographic puzzles [8].

5.8.2 Transaction Validation

Transaction is the essential building block in the Bitcoin network. Validated transactions are broadcasted to the nodes of a network. Many transactions altogether form a block. Many blocks are cryptographically linked to form a chain. Blocks are also verified before these are added to the chain. The validation and consensus procedures are carried out by mining nodes to validate a block. As shown in Fig. 5.8, each and every node has shared ledger. In order to make a transaction happen, for every node when it joins blockchain, it provides a wallet and a private key based on the provided identity of the individual node. As shown in Fig. 5.8, if Alice wants to transfer money to Bob in Bitcoin network, it needs to process a sequence of steps as shown in Fig. 5.9.

Every full node in the network validates the transactions by performing user authentication and data integrity. User authentication is ensured by decrypting the digital signature of the proposing user with the corresponding public key. Data integrity is checked by hashing the transaction data and comparing it with the decrypted signature. This procedure is followed for validating the transaction. Valid transactions accumulated in pool of valid transactions. The valid transactions are then broadcasted to the mining nodes in order to set up a new block in the network.

5.8.3 Mining and Block Structure

Miner gathers valid transactions and forms Merkle root hash using hashing mechanism. Merkle root header is then added to block header. In this way, all the valid transactions are pooled into a block. The number of transactions per block can be determined by the mining nodes. This block is then broadcasted to the mining nodes. To identify the next block in the network, consensus mechanisms are then utilized in the blockchain. Block generator/miner in the network mines the block based on the consensus. Miners compete with each other to solve a difficult mathematical puzzle like PoW. The miner verifies and validates the block by checking the correctness of block hash, block height and size values, previous block hash values, the validity of all transactions in the block, and the block timestamp values. After mining, miners are rewarded with fees. Upon successful mining, transaction fees are given from all the transaction nodes included in the block to the miner. The blockchain network also provides new coins when each new block is added to the chain.

Block structure contains the fields as shown in Fig. 5.10. To generate block header hash value for a block, six fields are required, namely, timestamp, difficulty

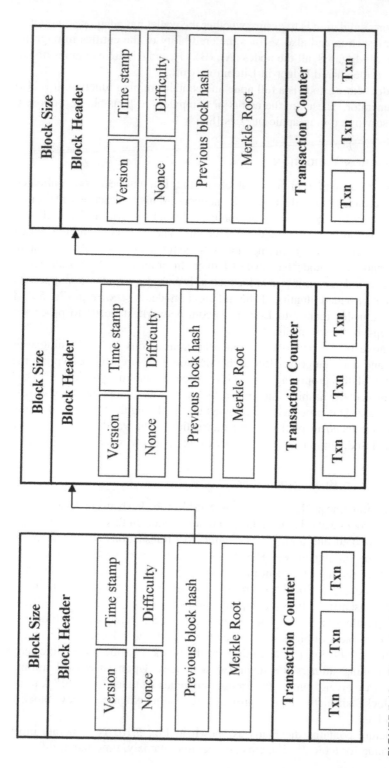

FIGURE 5.10   Block structure.

value, nonce, previous hash, Merkle root, and version. Generated hash number is checked with the target value set by the blockchain holders. If the generated hash value is less than the target value, the miner is considered as won and he will get the reward. If not, the nonce value has to be modified and the hash value to be generated again. Hence, it is a computational problem that picks random Nonce value and generates hash until the target is achieved. A measure of how difficult it is to find a block header hash value is called mining difficulty. The difficulty value in network changes for every 2016 blocks. If the difficulty value is increased, the number of iterations to attain the target will be increased. Block structure also maintains the size of the block, transaction counter, and transactions added in the block along with the block header. Every block is linked to previous block using the hash value of the previous block.

5.8.4 Consensus Mechanisms

Consensus is an agreement among full node on further block of transactions to be included in the blockchain. Extensive verification and validation process along with complex computation takes place to satisfy the agreement by the network entity. It ensures integrity of the network. The famous consensus algorithms are PoW, Proof of Stake (PoS), and Practical Byzantine Fault Tolerance (PBFT). In addition, there are several other consensus mechanisms such as Proof of Authority (PoA), Proof of Elapsed Time (PoET), Proof of Capacity (PoC), and so on. Different consensus protocols are chosen for various blockchain applications depending on the network needs and constraints.

PoW is a common consensus mechanism used in many popular blockchain-based applications like Bitcoin. PoW is famous because of the Bitcoin network. But it is not specific to cryptocurrency. Ethereum network followed Bitcoin to use PoW with slight modification. Ethereum metropolis protocol uses memory-based PoW which is not energy intensive. Every node that is trying to add block to blockchain has to crack some computational problems when PoW is the consensus involved in blockchain. Whoever solves the cryptographic puzzle first wins the consensus and will add the block to blockchain and also they get rewards in terms of crypto-currencies. The complexity of the puzzle depends on the factors such as network size, number of active users, blockchain size, and so on. As PoW fully depends on calculating the hash of block header elements by modifying nonce repeatedly, guessing and manipulating the hash of all nodes in a very short time span to hack the chain is impractical. PoW is computationally intensive to solve the puzzle. It results in enormous power consumption and requires longer processing time. But huge energy spent from non-winning node gets wasted. In PoW, the process of solving the cryptographic puzzle is called mining. When there are "n" nodes present in the blockchain and more than n/2 nodes are malicious nodes, blockchain hacking becomes possible. This attack is called 51% attack. Irrespective of the minor boundaries, PoW works well in many successful blockchain applications.

PoS is an alternative to PoW since its mining process uses enormous amount of electricity and computations to secure the network. The basic idea of PoW is to compete with each other nodes through mining process. Instead, PoS uses election process in which one particular node is randomly chosen to validate the next block. PoS has no miners and has validators. A node to become validators, the user must store some cryptocurrency as stake. The size of the stake determines the likelihood of the validators to be elected to add the next block. This process is called minting or forging. PoS don't need expensive mining equipment to add the block. Though 51% attack is less likely to happen in PoS, the algorithm also has to be cautious when choosing validators to choose the next block. It cannot be completely random and also stake alone is not sufficient to choose next validators as it might favor rich nodes frequently.

In distributed application, Byzantine Generals Problem states that group of generals may have communication problems when trying to agree a consensus due to system failures. In blockchain, each general represents a network node and they need to meet consensus on the current state of the system. This means that the majority of the system participants have to agree and execute the same action in order to achieve consensus. Byzantine Fault Tolerance (BFT) system is derived from Byzantine Generals Problem and BFT is able to keep on functioning, although some of the nodes fail to communicate or act maliciously. The aim of the BFT is to defend against the system failures by reducing the power of fake nodes. Practical Byzantine Fault Tolerance (pBFT) is an optimized BFT algorithm and it is used in many blockchain applications along with other consensus methods [9].

5.8.5 SMART CONTRACTS

In blockchain, smart contracts have been introduced in Ethereum framework. Smart contract is a business logic written as tiny computer program and stored in blockchain network. Contract is a written agreement between two or more parties that is intended to be enforced by law. Once the contract is deployed to blockchain, it is immutable. It cannot be stopped or modified. It is a protocol that creates an automated trustworthy set of rules mutually which is agreed upon between the parties. Solidity is a smart contract programming language, specifically created for Ethereum blockchain. This programming structure is similar to JavaScript. In decentralized systems, major issue is trust. Smart contracts help establish constraints to ensure trust between the parties of the network. It is similar to that of the "if-then" rules that are there in typical programming languages.

5.9 BLOCKCHAIN PLATFORMS

Blockchain concepts are implemented and tested in different platforms such as Ethereum, Hyperledger, Ripple, and so on. Each of them is created for executing specific types of blockchain categories.

5.9.1 ETHEREUM

Vitalik Buterin designed the Ethereum framework in order to apply decentralization to other fields other than money transferring purposes. The main aim of the framework is to run and build applications that could run globally without any central controlling authority. Ethereum is a public blockchain platform that enables developers to build and deploy decentralized applications.

Application that is executed on P2P network is called distributed application (DApp). Ethereum focuses on producing DApp with its features. DApps are decentralized applications that are not controlled by any authorities, rather it is controlled by the contracts written and deployed over the blockchain network. Every client in DApp interacts directly with its own instances of the DApp.

Developers program smart contracts using Ethereum languages. It is compiled, deployed, and run on Ethereum Virtual Machine (EVM). The smart contract code is verified by the nodes and all full nodes have a copy of the smart contract with them. If person A wants to transact money to person B, person A initiates and submits the work on blockchain for evaluation. Each node evaluates the work of person A. Upon successful verification, the transaction will be made and it is transparent to all the nodes. The smart contract code cannot be tampered once it is deployed on blockchain.

The smart contract code is compiled into byte code and loaded to EVM. EVM starts and executes transactions when the client is started. EVM also guarantees security against cyber-attacks. For every user in Ethereum, the Ethereum address is the identity and the private key of the user is the password. The wallets are software plugins used to store and manage Ethereum accounts. Ethereum account is the combination of Ethereum address and private key. Ethereum address is generated by forming the public key from private key of the user and calculating the hash value of public key using keccak256 and picking the last 20 bytes of the hashed value.

Cost is associated with each transaction. Like Bitcoin, Ethereum is P2P digital currency. The number of ethers to be paid for a transaction is based on the resources used. A transaction to add two numbers requires three units of work. This unit of work is called gas. Gas price is the price per unit gas. It is fixed by user. Miners will pick the transactions with higher gas price. Transaction fee is calculated by multiplying gas with gas price spent for a transaction. Gas limit indicates the maximum amount of gas a user willing to buy to execute the transaction.

Bitcoin Vs. Ethereum

- Bitcoin is a blockchain-based cryptocurrency. Ethereum is decentralized programming platform with smart contracts and tokens.
- Bitcoin is designed for financial transactions. Ethereum focuses on other data maintenance using smart contract codes.
- Bitcoin uses PoW consensus and Ethereum uses PoS or PoW consensus.
- Bitcoin takes 332 M transactions per day, whereas Ethereum takes 455 transactions per day. Average block size in Bitcoin is 767 KB and for Ethereum the maximum block size is 27 KB. The number of blocks in Bitcoin is 564 K. The number of blocks in Ethereum is 7.23 M.
- Bitcoin takes 10 minutes for mining and Ethereum takes 10–20 seconds. Bitcoin uses SHA-256 for hashing and Ethereum uses Ethash and keccak256.

FIGURE 5.11 Ganache blockchain testnet.

Framework Overview

The application can be developed and tested in a Truffle environment. A local blockchain network instance can be created using Ganache (a part of Truffle Suite). RPC server, network ID, gas limit, and gas price for the blockchain are set here. The addresses and the value for each address are preset for testing purposes as shown in Fig. 5.11.

The accounts can be loaded to the metamask from which the blockchain can be accessed as shown in Fig. 5.12.

Truffle framework provides required dependencies used for compiling a smart contract. The command "npx truffle unbox react" in the project directory installs all dependencies for solidity and React.js. From the generated directories, a Create React App is generated in the Client's directory. The project contracts are to be saved in the Contracts Directory as shown in Fig. 5.13.

The smart contracts are compiled using the command "Truffle compile". Then the Application Binary Interface (ABI) of the compiled contracts are generated. The contracts are pushed into the blockchain network. The directory of ABIs generated and port number for the blockchain networks are to be set in "truffle-config.js". The command "Truffle migrate" is executed to deploy the network. The front end for the application could be developed using React.js provided by the Truffle box. The web3.js provides collection of libraries that helps communicate the Blockchain node. [10].

5.9.2 HYPERLEDGER

Hyperledger is an open-source permissioned, private blockchain hosted by Linux foundation. It has no concept of cryptocurrency. It is designed for business-to-business applications. Private blockchain is suitable for the applications such as

FIGURE 5.12 Metamask.

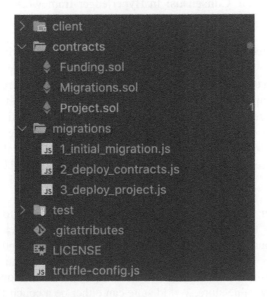

FIGURE 5.13 Project directory.

supply chain, aviation, banking, and so on. Hyperledger has frameworks such as Iroha, Sawtooth, Fabric, Indy, and Burrow. It also has tools such as Hyperledger Composer, Hyperledger Cello, Hyperledger Quilt, and Hyperledger Explorer. Framework and tools collectively build a blockchain application for several domains. Blockchain is not only meant for cryptocurrencies. So after Bitcoin, Ethereum came into the picture with the concept of smart contract to implement business logic and every transaction was also made public. In an enterprise market, the major objective of a system is to hide transactions from outside world or fellow nodes. So as to provide privacy in transactions among network entities, the private blockchain like Hyperledger Fabric was introduced.

Channels: Private blockchain approach is applied in Hyperledger using channel concept. Channel defines permissioned network of entities with single, common ledger for all its transactions and state changes. Even within channels data and transactions confidentiality can be achieved using cryptographic methods.

Assets: It represents tangible items or values that are transacted in the blockchain. Assets are represented as <key, value> pairs in JSON or Binary format.

Chaincode: Chaincode provides functions for performing on the transacted assets. It implements application-specific rules and policies on the network.

Ledger: Chaincode execution may result in state changes that are recorded in ledger. It maintains tamper-proof record of channel transactions.

Peers: Peers are the participant nodes that initiate transactions and maintain the state of the ledger. There are three major types of peers: endorsing peers, ordering peers, and committing peers. Endorsing peers receive and validate the transactions. It then signs them and returns to creating applications. Ordering peers collect the signed transactions, order them into blocks, and send them to committing peers. Committing peers validate conditions such as double spending, signatures, and then commit them to ledger.

Hyperledger Fabric Consensus: In Hyperledger framework, the consensus is achieved using the three consecutive mechanisms called endorse, order, and validate.

Ordering Service: It is responsible for packing the transaction into different blocks.

Membership Providers (MSP): It manages memberships and roles. The entities who want to participate in the Fabric network has to enroll in a trusted MSP. An organization manages its membership and the roles of the participating entities. These participating entities should have verifiable identity for realizing the trust. Implementation of MSP uses x.509 certificate as a digital identity. It determines the permissions for accessing the resources in blockchain network [11].

Client and Ledger Interaction: Client application is external to the blockchain network that sends transaction request to the network. Developer develops client application and smart contract. Communication between client and smart contract/ Chaincode happens over client SDK. The transaction request can either querying (get) or invoking (put and delete) transactions. Queries are responded by looking into world state key value store. World state can either be a couch DB or level DB.

Put and delete operations make an impact both in world state and ledger. At the end of the transactions, event is emitted. A peer contains a blockchain and world state. Frequently transacted data reside in world state which help increase throughput.

5.9.3 POLKADOT NETWORK

Blockchain applications are useful for improving open access and financial services with proper security enhancements. It is applied for various applications such as gaming, supply chain, Internet of Things and logistics, and so on. Single blockchain can only process limited number of transactions. When the number of transactions per second increases, a bottleneck occurs, and it also leads to increased transaction fees. There is a need for scaling up the existing blockchain method by devising the blockchain architecture for specific purposes that combines multiple chains and works together efficiently and securely. Polkadot is a Parachain network protocol that unites various diverse blockchain networks into one decentralized network. It makes blockchain scalable and customizable. It ensures cross-chain communications and transparent governance among multiple networks. It helps out upgrading the blockchain according to the need of application; hence, it is helpful for the developers, startups, and enterprises to make efficient use of blockchain technology. Relay chain is the core of the Polkadot network as all the blockchains are connected to it. It helps increase scalability by allowing transactions from all chains in the network at the same time. This simultaneous processing is called parallel chains. Cross-chain communication scheme allows any type of message transfer among the entities; hence interoperability is achieved. Blockchain may diverge into two separate paths while upgrading. This problem is called forking. Polkadot ensures forkless blockchain upgrading [12].

5.10 EDGE COMPUTING WITH BLOCKCHAIN

Blockchain can establish a secure and trusted resource allocation and sharing environment for IoT devices. It helps enhance the interoperability, reliability, security, and privacy of the systems by offloading the computations on edge devices. Blockchain network provides trusted resource allocation and sharing environment for IoT devices.

5.10.1 INTERNET OF THINGS AND BLOCKCHAIN

Internet of Things is collection of sensors or electronic/mechanical things that helps communicate with one another without human intervention. Since IoT devices have resource constraints to perform data analytics in itself, cloud systems were introduced. Though the objective is to build P2P systems, the intervention of cloud makes the system behave like centralized client server system. So, scalability of the system is affected. The IoT devices are designed by different vendors. Hence, heterogeneity in IoT devices causes interoperability issues. As IoT devices have resource constraints, providing authentication, authorization, and communication encryption kind of resource-intensive tasks may not be possible. They are done at cloud servers. If IoT devices are prone to security vulnerabilities, the firmware is updated to resolve it. Most of the times, it is left to the user who is responsible to update firmware. It becomes a security threat if he left it undone.

To overcome these challenges, IoT computation offloading is introduced with the help of edge devices where the processing can also be done. Blockchain when integrated with these edge devices, it can deal with poor interoperability, privacy, and security vulnerabilities, and hence improves heterogeneity [13].

Advantages of Combining IoT and Blockchain

- Interoperability of IoT systems is enhanced by storing heterogeneous IoT device data in blockchain. It enables universal Internet access for fragmented IoT networks.
- Security of IoT systems is improved. The transaction data or sensor readings are encrypted, digitally signed, and stored in blockchain.
- A smart contract in blockchain is written for updating firmware for ensuring security of IoT devices.
- Immutability of IoT devices is guaranteed by integrating blockchain. Consequently reliability of the data is accomplished.
- By leveraging the blockchain, IoT systems enable secure and trustless messaging between devices in IoT networks. As a consequence, an autonomic interaction of IoT is achieved by integrating smart contract to facilitate DAO.

Applications of Blockchain Integrated IoT Systems

- A refrigerator autonomously manages its interactions with the external world. Various sensors are available in refrigerator in order to control the operations and alarm user. Think about the refrigerator which is able to order the food based on the items and stock available in it and it automatically places order and pay for it. Typical actuators and sensors are alone not adequate for making it happen. Hence, IoT devices to be incorporated with smart contracts and payments must be made in a secure way.
- If some parts of the car are not functioning or got repaired what if it is smart enough to find and choose the best deal for parts and services. Blockchain can be integrated into connected cars to function more intelligently.

5.10.2 System Design

The IoT devices can be connected to the blockchain using centralized or decentralized model. In centralized model, Ethereum full node maintains full blockchain. All the IoT devices send data to the full node and the node verifies the smart contracts. Thus, IoT devices are under the control of Ethereum full node. Even though the blockchain mechanism is decentralized, the full node controls the IoT data. When the full node fails, the IoT devices cannot access the Blockchain network as it can be accessed only through the full node. This problem is resolved using RPC end point as shown in Fig. 5.14. IoT devices can individually access the smart contracts of blockchain through RPC end point. Application Binary Interface

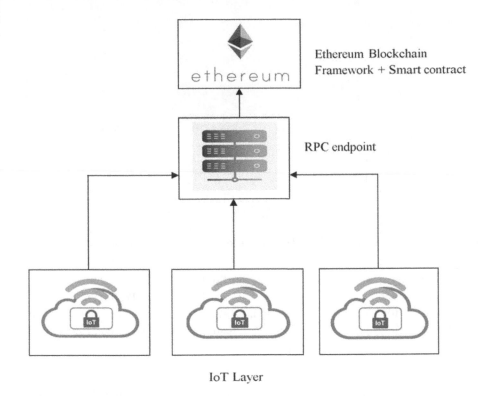

Ethereum Blockchain
Framework + Smart contract

RPC endpoint

IoT Layer

FIGURE 5.14 Blockchain integrated IoT devices.

(ABI) provides interface to the smart contract through web3 Ethereum API using RPC end point. ABIs of the contracts are exposed through the web3 API and web3 API is connected to RPC end point. Hence, RPC interface is providing communication between smart contract and web3 API. Decentralization is achieved using this approach.

5.10.3 Case Studies

Case Study I: Blockchain and IoT-Based Crowd Funding System

This system allows users to explore and fund project ideas published by project owners. The project owners and users use NFC Tags for their Hardware wallets used for funding and transactions. The users can log into the application and pay with the accounts associated with their NFC Tags. A "Funding" contract is deployed to the blockchain on which the project owners publish their project details for users to view. A smart contract is deployed for each project published which stores the current state information of the funding of the project such as the funding state and the amount of funds received so far. This contract checks the state of the contract (fundraising, successful, or expired) periodically whenever the application is running. If the state is successful, the funds are transferred from the contract to

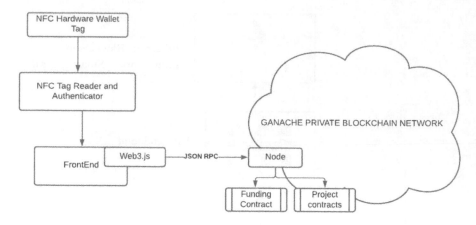

FIGURE 5.15   Architecture for blockchain and IoT-based crowd funding system.

the project owner. If the state is expired, the funds are returned to the users. The contract can accept payments. The system is developed using Truffle environment using web3.js for JSON RPC connection, React.js for the frontend, and Ganache CLI Private Blockchain Network used for testing. The NFC authentication and processing is done using python nfcpy library (Fig. 5.15) [14].

Smart Contracts Using Solidity Language

Two smart contracts were used for the development of the application. A "Funding" smart contract instance can have many "Project" smart contracts associated with it.

Funding Contract   The following function starts a project with the parameters sent from the frontend through web3 and deploys a project contract and pushes the contract to the list of projects associated with this Funding Contract.

```
function startProject(
string calldata title,
string calldata description,
uint durationInDays,
uint amountToRaise
) external {
uint raiseUntil = block.timestamp + (durationInDays *
(1 days));
Project   newProject   =   new   Project(msg.sender,
amountToRaise, raiseUntil, title, description);
projects.push(newProject);
emit ProjectStarted(
address(newProject),
```

```
msg.sender,
title,
description,
raiseUntil,
amountToRaise
);
}
```

The following function returns all the projects associated with the instance of the funding contract:

```
function returnAllProjects() external view returns
(Project[] memory) {
return projects;
}
```

Project Contract

Contribution Function which is called when the user enters a value to contribute:

```
function contribute() external verifyProjectState
(ProjectState.FundRaising) payable {
require (msg.sender != projectOwner);
contributions[msg.sender] = contributions[msg.sender]
+ (msg.value);
currentBalance = currentBalance + (msg.value);
emit FundingReceived(msg.sender, msg.value,
currentBalance);
checkFundingState();
}
```

Function to check the state of the project contract:

```
function checkFundingState() public{
if(currentBalance >= amountGoal){
currentState = ProjectState.successful;
payProjectOwner();
}
else if(block.timestamp > deadLine){
currentState = ProjectState.expired;
}
}
```

Function that pays the address which creates that specific project contract when the goal is reached:

```
function payProjectOwner() internal verifyProject-
State(ProjectState.successful) returns(bool){
uint256 raisedAmount = currentBalance;
currentBalance = 0;
if(projectOwner.send(raisedAmount)){
emit ProjectOwnerPaid(projectOwner);
return true;
}
else{
currentBalance = raisedAmount;
currentState = ProjectState.successful;
return false;
}
}
```

Case Study II: Biometric System with Blockchain Technology

Blockchain technology provides the suitable architecture to store and retrieve sensitive and confidential data in a secure and decentralized system. Biometrics can be one among those data which can make use of the blockchain features such as immutability, better security, and decentralized system. Automated recognition of a person with the use of biometric traits integrated with blockchain can help in securing the smart devices in many IOT applications. Biometric traits can be either physiological (face, fingerprint, and so on) or behavioral (voice, handwritten sign, and so on).

Issues with Existing System

When the biometrics is stored in a single centralized database, attackers can steal the biometrics and leak them, which may have greater consequences. In case of a password theft, it is easy to change and replace the password. The attacker can also modify the stored biometrics resulting in authentication failure. These issues can be resolved using blockchain technology to store the biometrics, as it is secure and tamper-proof from security attacks.

Design Considerations

Biometrics is private and sensitive information. When a variable in smart contract is declared as private, it only means that the variable cannot be accessed from another smart contract but can be read by external APIs like web3. So, the biometrics cannot be simply stored as anyone can access and view those data. One way to solve this issue is to encrypt the data before storing it in the blockchain and decrypt it during authentication. In recent days, homomorphic encryption is getting quite popular as it allows one to perform the calculation on the encrypted data and giving the same results obtained by performing the calculation after decrypting the data.

Each instruction executed in Ethereum requires the payment of certain amount of gas (cryptocurrency). Simple addition instruction can cost 1 gas, while other complex calculations like the calculation of SHA3 hash can cost 30 gas. Hence, most of the computations such as feature extraction, encryption, and feature comparison should be done outside the smart contract.

System Design

1. **Feature extraction from biometric data**
   Biometrics of a person is generated using various sensors. For example, to use face as the biometric trait, cameras can be used to capture the face of a person and extract the features from the captured image.
2. **Storing the encrypted data**
   The biometrics cannot be stored directly in the blockchain as anyone can read the biometrics. Deploying the biometric system in public blockchain is more safe and secure than using private blockchain as it allows only a small number of trusted users to participate in the network. By incorporating suitable encryption algorithm, the features are encrypted and stored in the public blockchain.
3. **Feature comparison and authentication**

During authentication, the user's biometrics are captured, features are extracted and compared against the data stored in the blockchain. The comparison is done by calculating the distance (Euclidean or Hamming) between the two biometrics and finally user is authenticated when the biometric matches.

System Implementation

A simple biometric system using facial features is implemented to test the system. A python package called face_recognition is used to generate the face encoding of a person and encrypt the feature vector using AES256 algorithm. Then, the encrypted text is stored in the blockchain network (enrollment). The text is retrieved and decrypted during the authentication process. The smart contract deployed in the network is given below.

Smart Contract

```
pragma solidity >=0.4.22 <0.8.0;
contract Face {
//The encrypted face encodings are stored in a mapping
with address as mapping key
mapping(address => string) private faceEncoding;
address public admin;
constructor()
{
admin=msg.sender;
}
function addFace(address adr,string memory face)
public
{
//Only the admin (address used to deploy the smart con-
tract) has the privilege to add the face encoding
require(admin==msg.sender);
faceEncoding[adr]=face;
}
function getFace(address adr) public view returns
(string memory)
{
return faceEncoding[adr];
}
}
```

The processing capability in Ethereum is slow as it can process only 10–12 transactions per second, which reduces its usability for biometric system. The scalability is also one other important challenge to consider during larger implementation. Despite its limitations, biometrics integrated with blockchain has great potential. The biometrics when stored in centralized database has high threat to security attacks and alterations. With blockchain in picture, better security and immutability can be achieved (Fig. 5.16).

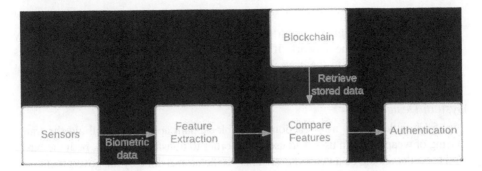

FIGURE 5.16 System design for biometrics system with blockchain.

Case Study III: Weapon Tracking Using Blockchain

Introduction

Possession of a gun or any other firearm could lead to unnecessary violence and may disturb the public. Misuse of guns can result in public nuisance and harmful deaths. The significant reason for gun-related violence is due to improper tracking of ownership. Firearms and dangerous weapons in the hands of many people may have its effect in suicides and murders. The buying and selling of weapons need to be streamlined to control the illegal usage of these harmful weapons. DLT with cryptography backbone plays a vital role in gun control without making any changes to existing law and orders. Blockchain is such a technology that will improve the tracking of the gun and ownership. The owner will be accountable for any crime found with those weapons. The distributed ledger can be used for immutable record keeping for gun distribution process and ownership rights. Every individual user will have sufficient data that will help to analyze the background check. The data might include previous gun-related crimes, suicide attempts, and so on. That adds to the credibility score of the user. Government bodies responsible for weapon possession and licensing can either have partial or entire access to these immutable records.

Functionalities

1. **Background check**
   Blockchain is immutable and less vulnerable to hacking and human error; as a result, all the data and previous transactions made by the user will remain intact. These data can be used to make the background check. This check is essential to pass the validation for transferring the ownership as well as to provide the license to the user to possess the firearms.
2. **Tracking manufacturers and sale of weapons**
   Weapons are tracked from the manufacturer to the resale. Illegal weapons found during crime scenes can be easily tracked to their manufacturers as well the current and previous owners. Illegal smuggling of weapons can be identified. By tracking the health data of owners, users with poor mental fitness can be traced, which helps to prevent suicides.

3. **Data sharing**

Since the system is decentralized, any user can try to sell weapons to any other users in the network. If the buyer fails to pass the verification, then this can be notified to the government bodies and authorities to further prevent any unforeseen situations.

System Design

Fig. 5.17 explains how a transaction in the blockchain application will aid the transferring of weapons from user A to user B. In order to transfer a weapon, both the buyer and the seller should be a verified user. This verification is done by the government who are also a part of the blockchain network. The users will undergo the background check and validity of the license provided by the government bodies in the network. If the user does not own a license, then the user is eligible to make a request transaction to obtain a license provided the user successfully passes through all the verification and validation. If the user meets the eligibility criteria to obtain the firearm, then the government body will validate all the previous records and transactions made by the user.

Every user in the blockchain who sells or purchases guns will have an electronic gun safe that is tied to the biometric data of the user such as fingerprints. The electronic gun safe will contain the records of the user's mental issues if any and other history of illegal activities. The safe also contains all the previous transactions and the ballistic information of various guns possessed. All the previous records and transactions made by the user are immutable in the blockchain. These data are stored in the respective nodes that the government authorities are entitled to access. The data are

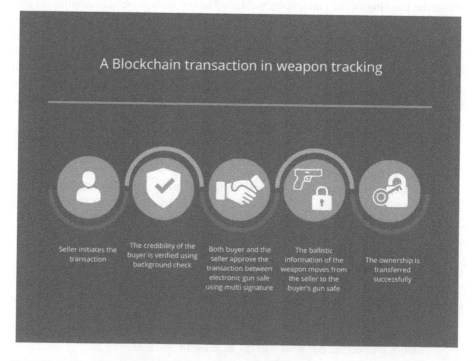

FIGURE 5.17   Blockchain transaction in weapon tracking.

hidden from other nodes in the network concerning the privacy of the user. If the personal identity of the user possessing weapons is public then there are high chances of subjugation. The biometric data of the user can be used as a private key to access the personal data in the electronic gun safe. Only during transfer of ownership, these data are verified as a background check. Artificial intelligence can be employed to identify any mental issues or any obsession toward gun violence.

All the transaction will require parties at both the end to approve the sale which is done using multisignature technology (multisig). Multisig will enable both licensed and verified buyer and seller to sign using respective keys. Once the buyer is verified and passes the background check, there is transfer of data from seller's electronic safe to buyers safe. This transaction between the electronic guns safe is recorded in the immutable blockchain and is also timestamped. If the receiver of the gun fails to pass the background check, then the same will also be recorded in its own electronic gun safe for future validation.

Implementation

A smart contract is written with the help of Remix online IDE for simulating the application. Though the smart contract does not meet all the specifications that were mentioned earlier, it promises to provide an overview of how the application would be if it is implemented in the real world.

```solidity
pragma solidity ^0.5.0;
contract Weapons {
// A structure to hold the details of the weapons
struct Weapon {
string name;
string physical_information;
string weapon_type;
}
// A structure to hold the details of the users
struct User {
string name;
mapping(uint=>Weapon) owned;
uint count;
uint trust_level;
}
//A table to store the users
mapping(uint=>User) users;
// A table to store the weapons
mapping(uint=>Weapon) weapons;
// Validates the credibility of the user
function validate(uint id) public returns(uint) {
users[id].trust_level = 1;
```

```
}
// Invalidate the user if a malicious activity is
discovered
function invalidate(uint id) public {
users[id].trust_level -= 1;
}
// Adds the weapon to the buyer and removes the weapon
from the seller
function transaction(uint id1, uint id2, uint weapon)
public {
if(validate(id1)==1 && validate(id2)==1) {
Weapon memory temp = users[id1].owned[weapon];
delete users[id1].owned[weapon];
users[id2].owned[weapon] = temp;
users[id1].count--;
users[id2].count++;
}
}
// A function to add the users into the blockchain
function addUser(uint id, string memory name) public {
users[id].name = name;
users[id].count = 0;
validate(id);
}
// A function to buy weapons from manufacturer
function requestWeapon(uint id, uint wid) public {
if(validate(id)==1) {
users[id].owned[wid] = weapons[wid];
users[id].count = 1;
}
else {
invalidate(id);
}
}
// A function to add guns that are manufactured
function addGun(uint wid, string memory name, string
memory physical_information, string memory weap-
on_type) public {
weapons[wid].name = name;
weapons[wid].physical_information = physical_
information;
weapons[wid].weapon_type = weapon_type;
}
}
```

Blockchain will serve to control the sales and usage of guns and other harmful weapons. It tracks the gun flow from manufacturer to the end user. Every gun is linked to an individual who owns the gun. The blockchain protocol will efficiently implement the existing legal laws of possession of firearms without the need for any modification. All the data are immutable and the system keeps track of all the previous transactions of users which will come in aid during the background check. This reduces the extensive need of the workforce as well as minimizes the time taken to track the data of a user. This might help in controlling interpersonal violence and suicides as the owner of the weapons are tracked and any crime identified is recorded. Any inappropriate or offensive remarks in the records will only affect the credibility of the user to buy weapons in the future. The application will help the government body to track the crime and legitimacy of the user when providing the license.

5.11 RESEARCH CHALLENGES AND FUTURE RESEARCH DIRECTIONS

- Research on the computation offloading of IoT device data with the help of Blockchain technology drastically improves the security and privacy of the data in a decentralized platform. Smart contracts can help define rules for handling the data in an effective manner.
- Blockchain is not completely secure from certain vulnerabilities. Smart contracts when written and deployed cannot be modified. Hence, smart contract errors or faults may lead to vulnerabilities like DAO attack. Various research works can be incorporated to blockchain to prevent these attacks.
- Exploring various incentive mechanisms and consensus mechanisms improves the quality of blockchain.
- The data stored in blockchain are in an encrypted form. Exploiting big data analysis on encrypted data is still under research.
- The number of transactions is reduced due to the computationally intensive consensus mechanisms. The scalability of the system can be enhanced by inculcating less computational intensive consensus mechanisms or by designing consortium blockchain network.

EXPERT NOTES BY DR. BITHIN ALANGOT, RESEARCH ASSISTANT, SINGAPORE UNIVERSITY OF TECHNOLOGY AND DESIGN

I got introduced into the blockchain technology while designing a framework called HPlane for remote healthcare monitoring systems. Our framework allows for efficient management of healthcare data such that the amount of data transferred between different distributed entities in the system is optimized. However, managing the access control models is too complex since the framework is used by multiple untrusted entities. Thus, blockchain technology severs as the perfect solution that can overcome the challenges with respect to access control in HPlane. But blockchain integration is not straightforward since (1) it can lead to privacy concerns and prone to eclipse attack, and (2) it does not scale well. Thus, the first work was to solve the scalability issues in blockchain which uses PBFT as the underlying consensus protocol. Later, I worked toward finding a solution to detect eclipse attacks on blockchain clients by designing a ubiquitous gossip protocol. This work was done in collaboration with researchers at Singapore University of Technology and Design.

Another two interesting research works that I carry out with blockchain are (1) SmartWitness: Securing software supply chain using blockchain, and (2) Decentralized Identity Authentication with auditability and privacy. In the first project, the main objective was to use blockchain to prevent malicious software distribution. The system was built on the Ethereum blockchain platform, and the opportunity of being part of the project helped to build my expertise in blockchain. While the second project was toward solving an issue with Decentralized Identity (DID), a blockchain-based identity system. Our solution enables a user who owns a DID to detect if any malicious entity used his identity without knowledge. However, the challenge was in providing privacy since our solution relies on blockchains and any data on blockchain is publicly visible. We used a zero-knowledge succinct argument of knowledge (ZK-SNARK) and Verifiable Random Function (VRF) primitives to achieve privacy properties.

The research on Decentralized Identity system using blockchain is still in its earlier stages and I am excited to contribute my idea to the community. Currently, I specifically look at verifiable credentials, zero-knowledge proofs, and identity-based encryption schemes.

5.12 SUMMARY

The IoT device when integrated to smart systems monitors and observes its functionalities without human interventions. Though it provides immense benefits to the system, there are certain shortcomings. The IoT devices generate massive data which actually handled by cloud servers. Real-time processing systems must provide response with minimized latency. Pushing data to cloud and processing over there delays the entire servicing time. Hence, edge devices are designed so as to provide the computations near to the source of the data. Edge devices are capable of handling real-time data and the IoT-generated data can be offloaded to process and to make decisions on time. In order to provide guarantee for tamper-proof data transactions, blockchain architecture is proposed with these edge devices. It drastically increases the security and privacy of the IoT-generated data in the network. Based on the applications and requirements, the type of the blockchain and consensus mechanisms can be preferred. Introducing smart contracts in blockchain helps in implementing tiny logic on IoT data onboard using edge instead of pushing it to cloud.

REFERENCES

1. Ranjan, R., et al. (2018). The next grand challenges: Integrating the Internet of Things and data science. *IEEE Cloud Computing*, 5(3), 12–26.

2. Maull, R., et al. (2017). Distributed ledger technology: Applications and implications. *Strategic Change*, *26*(5), 481–489.
3. Zheng, Z., et al. (2017). An overview of blockchain technology: Architecture, consensus, and future trends. *2017 IEEE international congress on big data (BigData congress)*. IEEE.
4. Henry, R., Herzberg, A., & Kate, A. (2018). Blockchain access privacy: Challenges and directions. *IEEE Security & Privacy*, *16*(4), 38–45.
5. Anitha Kumari, K., Sudha Sadasivam, G., & Rohini, L. (2016). An efficient 3D elliptic curve Diffie-Hellman (ECDH) based two-server password-only authenticated key exchange protocol with provable security. *IETE Journal of Research*, *62*(6), 762–773.
6. Anitha Kumari, K., Padmashani, R., Varsha, R., & Upadhayay, V. (2020). Securing Internet of Medical Things (IoMT) using private blockchain network. In S. L. Peng, S. Pal, & L. Huang (Eds), *Principles of Internet of Things (IoT) ecosystem: Insight paradigm. Intelligent systems reference library* (Vol. 174, 305–326). Cham: Springer.
7. Liu, M., Wu, K., & Xu, J. J. (2019). How will blockchain technology impact auditing and accounting: Permissionless versus permissioned blockchain. *Current Issues in Auditing*, *13*(2), A19–A29.
8. Pazmiño, J. E., & Rodrigues, C. K. S. (2015). Simply dividing a bitcoin network node may reduce transaction verification time. *The SIJ Transactions on Computer Networks & Communication Engineering (CNCE)*, *3*(2), 17–21.
9. Zheng, Z., et al. (2017). An overview of blockchain technology: Architecture, consensus, and future trends. *2017 IEEE international congress on big data (BigData congress)*. IEEE.
10. Antonopoulos, A. M., & Wood, G. (2018). *Mastering ethereum: Building smart contracts and DApps*. O'Reilly Media.
11. Cachin, C. (2016). Architecture of the hyperledger blockchain fabric. *Workshop on Distributed Cryptocurrencies and Consensus Ledgers*, *310*(4). 1–4.
12. https://polkadot.network/technology/
13. Sharma, P. K., Chen, M.-Y., & Park, J. H. (2017). A software defined fog node based distributed blockchain cloud architecture for IoT. *IEEE Access*, *6*, 115–124.
14. Hartmann, F., et al. (2019). Alternative fundraising: Success factors for blockchain-based vs. conventional crowdfunding. *2019 IEEE international workshop on blockchain oriented software engineering (IWBOSE)*. IEEE.

6 Edge Computing Use Cases and Case Studies

6.1 USE CASES

Every organization must have a clear goal of data storage and its architecture to upkeep the planned use cases according to the priority/preference level. Organizations are required to analyze gamut of highly prospective use cases and its tendency to entice other stakeholders. Few sectors are described in this chapter that best utilize edge computing systems by highlighting the opportunities and point to ponder. Manifold ways exist to characterize the use cases and this chapter is limited with most commonly applied domains/sectors/applications. Healthcare sector case studies are presented elaborately in this chapter with a detailed illustration and working module.

6.2 EDGE COMPUTING HIGH-POTENTIAL USE CASES

High-potential use cases that drive the real world are elaborated in this section [1,2]. Few of the highly prospective use cases are discussed as follows:

- Autonomous vehicles
- Smart cities
- Industrial automation
- Network functions
- Gaming
- Content delivery
- Financial sector
- Augmented reality/virtual reality
- Healthcare sector

6.2.1 AUTONOMOUS VEHICLES

Many automotive industries started to invest dollars of money in a smart way in driverless cars using contemporary technologies. Though complete dependency on machines is not possible, operating safely is a better solution. To function efficiently, these vehicles are required to collect and analyze data from different orientations, surroundings, and climatic conditions. It should have the potential to decide on its own based on the previous experience/learning. In addition, present feedback/decisions taken by the vehicles need to send back to the nearest edge servers placed by the providers/manufacturers in order to operate effectively and to communicate with the local government bodies. The efficacy is based on the data

DOI: 10.1201/9781003230946-6

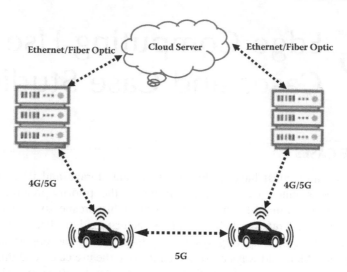

FIGURE 6.1 Autonomous vehicle communication.

collected and analyzed for providing alerts and communicating the information with nearby vehicles in the network with no inconsistency. The influx of data must be transmitted to the vehicles in the network with no lack in bandwidth and latency to offer high reliability in the edge-enabled environment. Edge-enabled autonomous vehicles must have the capability to learn things from past decisions and to make spontaneous onboard decisions using machine learning techniques like reinforcement learning. Autonomous vehicle functioning is shown in Fig. 6.1 for better understanding.

6.2.2 SMART CITIES

A massive amount of data is influx in Metropolitan cities from various sources such as individuals, buildings, vehicles, and devices with the help of sensors. The data are gathered, processed, analyzed, and managed for gaining insights and using the resources efficiently, thereby improving the functioning of the city in traffic, necessary home utilities, trash, anomaly detection, and other societal services. Existing schemes are deficient in providing an instantaneous response for taking immediate actions. As a repercussion, edge emerges to offer solution to things without any delay in network outskirts. Edge computing is a real-time permanent solution for this changing environment receiving requests from multitude of things. It provides a spotlight of people living condition and service utilization in metropolitan places. In the future, the connection among the devices/people/buildings will be proactive and reactive in nature. However, the level of collaboration among the people/devices may vary according to the situation. Multitude of things and intelligence merge together to make the place highly digitalized and interactive to live life in a better manner. Manifold initiatives are launched by companies like

Google, IBM, and Cisco to support the government in this project. For instance, IBM launched its smart city challenge to develop the urban ecosystem. This strategy is well adopted by many countries across the world to improve the lifestyle by focusing on e-services, sustaining novel ecosystems with high broadband networks. Universities like Tel Aviv join hands with this new venture with their focus on smart transportation by incorporating artificial intelligence with the ecosystem.

6.2.3 INDUSTRIAL AUTOMATION

Manufacturing industries are the prime benefiters of the fourth industrial revolution that is popularly known as Industry 4.0. With the tremendous growth of IoT devices and their management, the current generation is on the cusp of the fifth industrial revolution. Integration of data storage facilities and computing in industrial sector realizes the benefits such as minimum energy consumption and cost. The flattened edge architecture realizes energy efficiency and predictive maintenance in industrial sectors that in turn results in high production. Acquiring data from various sources and effective analysis aids the industries to become smart by increasing the production with customization as per customer requirements. In case of companies operating with low/poor bandwidth, edge computing is considered as an irreplaceable solution. Edge computing is a more suitable framework for industrial applications such as aircraft/missile launch, offshore oil rig, energy manufacturing, fraud detection, monitoring of logistics equipment, and so on. For instance, during missile launch edge framework must collect, analyze, and monitor data on various weather factors without depending upon remote data centers. The intelligent machine learning algorithms learn from past experience and process the data in judicious manner that ultimately results in improving the operational efficiency.

6.2.4 NETWORK FUNCTIONS

Due to the immense explosion of data and devices, every device is associated with an IP address for identity, communication, and traceability. Current network function is not suffice to upkeep the process efficiently as the interconnected devices consume large bandwidth. Edge gateway is considered as the best solution to reduce bandwidth consumption by placing it very close to the devices. Rationalizing the data at edge gateway enhances the effectiveness of overall function, especially bandwidth consumption. In contrast, improvisation processes/procedures must be applied on routers, firewalls, and switches to uphold the function either physically or virtually as it runs in cloud systems. Adaptation of these devices to the local actuation point, edge remains as a highest challenge as the rudimentary functions like security operations/rules and packet forwarding must function on onboard without outsourcing to cloud to improve the overall efficacy and performance. Many industries and researchers initiated work in this area to integrate network virtual functions in multi-access edge computing platforms.

6.2.5 GAMING

From youngsters to old age, many people around the world are drowned in video games. Though there is a negative impact on few games, it is proved that games providing abundant benefits to old age people in particular of brain functioning. In addition, it pulls down the negative mental effects and improves memory power. On the contrary, the games consume high bandwidth and latency sensitivity in a multi-player gaming environment. By placing edge servers close to the places, backhaul bandwidth and low latency are promising. The lower the latency, the better the gaming environment is guaranteed. With edge computing, better user experience is feasible and it reignites the user experience. Edge-hosted gaming service at an affordable price is another fortuning service offered to the users than investing a huge amount in PlayStation/Xbox.

6.2.6 CONTENT DELIVERY

Better experience is guaranteed for accessing a web page, video, or music via edge computing model as the response is ensured in milliseconds rather than depending upon the response from the cloud data center. The Content Delivery Network (CDN) market has been controlled/ruled by players, like Akamai and Limelight by significant construction of expansive networks. Few providers like Netflix/HBO sprawl their customized micro-cache at edge network with greater reliability and flexibility.

6.2.7 FINANCIAL SECTOR

To enable Smart Banking facility, banking sectors are adopting edge computing frameworks for better consumer experience and service. The service is offered via different multitudes over smartphone, desktop/laptop. In addition, the feature is expanded to ATMs and kiosks with the strong inbuilt functionality to collect and process data. With these wider ranges of features, banking sectors attract customers with much more responsive design. Edge computing supports trading sectors by speeding up the communication and computation, thus reduces the overall loss. High-speed execution is viable by placing the edge servers very close to stock exchanges to run high resource intensive protocols/algorithms. More accurate and appropriate latest information is facilitated to the providers and consumers with this high benefitted model.

6.2.8 AUGMENTED REALITY

Augmented reality pays recent attention due to its applicability in more common practical applications. Augmented reality facilitates a real appearance to the users by overlaying digital devices/elements on top of real-world objects/environments. Wearable devices such as headsets, glasses, smart watches, jackets, and rings create virtual effects most widely via smartphones. The most familiar application of augmented reality is the filter option in Instagram/Snapchat. The working procedure behind augmented reality necessitates the elements/devices to process visual data and to map the visual data to real-time objects. Edge framework works in a better lighter manner that allows devices to fuse with augmented reality displays spontaneously without any delay. Many retail chains are making use of this technology for a better shopping experience.

6.2.9 HEALTHCARE SECTOR

Edge computing fascinates health sectors by creating new opportunities to incorporate recent IT solutions for promising patient care. Gathering, protecting, and processing a humongous amount of patient data becomes real with the aid of edge computing. Dynamic real-time decisions and actions are possible to provide by the healthcare sectors even to the rural background people as e-services in milliseconds of time with the deployment of edge. In addition, anywhere, any time access to information is possible than depending upon one centralized database. Recently, many medical devices appear and ruling the market with a provision to collect and process data that plays a major role during treatment or diagnosis. For instance, simple prediction of heart disease using low-density lipoproteins in edge computing systems is proposed by Anitha Kumari et al. [3]. Thus, edge computing creates a huge impact on every person's daily life to lead a healthy and safe life.

Apart from this, edge computing lays its footprints in sectors/applications like video monitoring, video conferencing, software-defined networking, connecting homes and offices, and retail.

The realization of use cases in edge computing is presented in Fig. 6.2 for a clear understanding.

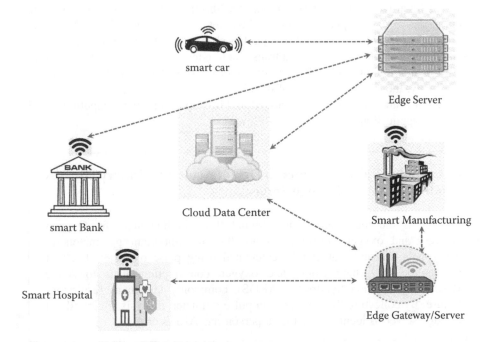

FIGURE 6.2 Realization of edge use cases.

6.3 REALIZATION OF EDGE COMPUTING IN HEALTHCARE ENSURING STORAGE SECURITY

The healthcare industry is one of the world's largest and fastest growing industries. Transforming healthcare into the digital era is predominant to reduce operational costs and provide better diagnostic tools for healthcare professionals by making digital patient data available in a timely fashion. Accessing the records dynamically at any point with low latency and hard-to-reach places realizes the highest usage of edge computing in real time. Generally, in healthcare records, patients often deal with missing or incorrect medical information when they happen to visit a new provider or facility. There are chances that the patient's data can be misused if hackers get access to it. Each and every information has to be monitored to avoid the occurrence of undesired events and also to prevent it from attacks. To store and protect the security and privacy of healthcare digital data, between the layers, several methods exist, such as attribute-based encryption, proxy re-encryption, functional encryption, honey encryption, and homomorphic encryption. Homomorphic encryption is the cutting edge cryptographic technique that allows computations to be carried out on an encrypted data than in plain text to provide privacy and data storage security similar to conventional cryptography, but with added capabilities like searching on encrypted data. Among many types, Fully Homomorphic Encryption (FHE) is widely used that allows full computation over encrypted data. FHE is an emerging cryptographic technique to permit computation on encrypted data without the need to bring the data back to the computational node [4,5].

Typically a transition requires personal health information is protected in three different phases of manipulation of digital patient data: (1) acquisition, (2) storage, and (3) computation. In these Case studies, data is gathered from Internet of Medical Things (IoMT) devices and transmits to edge gateway/server. Edge device stores the data homomorphically for further processing/analyzing upon encrypted data. Finally, the required portion of data is sent to the cloud server.

Three case studies have been discussed in this chapter for edge computing-based healthcare applications, which are as follows:

Case Study I Pulse Oximeter to Detect Acute Respiratory Distress Syndrome (ARDS) in Edge Server

Oxygen is the most important essential thing in human's life. Oxygen delivery and oxygen consumption are the two important parameters in everyone's life and that can be calculated using pulse oximeter. Lack of oxygen delivery, hemoglobin and oxygen consumption leads to Acute Respiratory Distress Syndrome (ARDS), commonly known as respiratory failure. By collecting these values via pulse oximeter, analysis is carried out in edge server to identify whether a person has ARDS or not.

Case Study II Blood Pressure to Determine Hypotension in Edge Server

Mean Arterial Pressure (MAP) is the average blood pressure in a person's blood vessels during a single cardiac cycle. Based on the systolic and diastolic value acquired via blood pressure monitor, MAP is computed and is analyzed in edge server to determine whether a person has hypotension or not.

Case Study III Body Composition Scale to Detect Heat Index in Edge Server

Body compositions are more important to be considered every day for human physical fitness that is calculated using body composition scale. An increase in humidity and indoor temperature leads to an increase in heat index that leads to many health problems. Based *on* humidity and temperature value from body composition scale, heat index is calculated and analyzed in edge server to identify the effects of heat index for the individual.

In order to facilitate secure storage of the private details and efficient prediction of ARDS, hypotension, and heat index, FHE schemes are integrated and analyzed in edge gateway/server.

6.3.1 DEVICES AND SETUP

To execute these case studies, blood pressure monitor, pulse oximeter, and body composition scale are considered. These devices are connected with Dell Edge Gateway 5100 series with the configuration as Intel Atom-E3825 CPU of 1.33 GHz, Ubuntu Core 16 OS, 2GB DDR3L-1067 MHz, and 32GB Solid State Hard Drive for efficient processing. Further, the gateway is connected to centralized cloud server.

6.3.2 CASE STUDY I: PULSE OXIMETER TO DETECT ARDS IN EDGE SERVER

In human's life, oxygen is necessary for respiration because the human body uses the oxygen to burn food molecules. Oxygen must be transported efficiently to the tissues from the atmosphere in order to maintain normal metabolism. For example, COVID-19 patients being admitted to hospitals report symptoms like not being able to think properly or taste or headaches, which happen because of higher concentration of CO_2 in the blood and cause damage to the lungs. In such cases, an oximeter can alert them. Pulse oximeter is a small, clip-like device that attaches to a body part commonly put on a finger. The purpose of pulse oximetry is to check how well your heart is pumping oxygen through your body. It may be used to monitor the health of individuals with any type of condition such as ARDS, chronic obstructive pulmonary disease (COPD), asthma, pneumonia, lung cancer, anemia, heart attack or heart failure, congenital heart defects which can affect blood oxygen levels. FHE schemes are used for encryption and make an analysis of encrypted data to predict whether the person is affected by ARDS or not.

Wu Suyu and Yi Weidong proposed a system in the year 2009 for routing the data from many nodes to a single receiving device. Two Medicare sensors, namely, heart beat sensors and pulse oximeter are interconnected in a network to collect heart beat and pulse oximeter values. The monitoring devices use an MSP430 microcontroller and LCD screen for displaying the values that are connected to WSN node via RS232 serial communication port to transmit to the edge gateway and finally to the cloud server [6].

6.3.2.1   Pulse Oximetry

Pulse oximetry is a simple and non-invasive method used to examine oxygen saturation (SpO_2) in various parts of body. Pulse oximetry is considered as a proper alternative to the patients for checking O_2 saturation as it reduces the frequency of bleeding during the analysis of arterial blood gases. Speed, convenient use, and high accuracy in continuous monitoring of patients and detection of hypoxia are other features of pulse oximetry. It detects the amount of oxyhemoglobin and deoxygenated hemoglobin in arterial blood to embody it as oxyhemoglobin saturation that is an indirect estimation of arterial oxygen saturation (SaO_2).

6.3.2.2   Oxygen Delivery (DO_2)

Global oxygen delivery (DO_2) is the amount of oxygen delivered to the whole body from the lungs [7,8]. It is the product of total blood flow or cardiac output (CO) and the oxygen content of arterial blood (CaO_2) and is usually expressed in ml min^{-1} and is described using the equation:

$$DO_2 = CO * CaO_2 \qquad (6.1)$$

The oxygen content of arterial blood (CaO_2) is described using the equation:

$$CaO_2 = (k1 \times Hb \times SaO_2) + (k2 \times PaO_2) \qquad (6.2)$$

where Hb is the hemoglobin concentration (g $liter^{-1}$), SaO_2 is the arterial Hb oxygen saturation, PaO_2 is arterial oxygen partial pressure, k1 is the Hufner's constant to denote the oxygen combining capacity of Hb and it varies from 1.34 to 1.39, and k2 is the quantity of dissolved oxygen in plasma. For our research, the value taken for k1 is 1.34 and k2 is 0.0031.

6.3.2.3 Oxygen Consumption (VO_2)

Global oxygen consumption (VO_2) is the volume of oxygen consumed by the tissues per minute [7,8]. Under aerobic conditions, oxygen is consumed to generate energy so that VO_2 corresponds to the metabolic rate and is described using the equation:

$$VO_2 = CO \times (CaO_2 - CvO_2) \tag{6.3}$$

The oxygen content of venous blood (CvO_2) is described using the equation:

$$CvO_2 = (k1 \times Hb \times SvO_2) + (k2 \times PvO_2) \tag{6.4}$$

where Hb is the hemoglobin concentration (g $liter^{-1}$), SvO_2 is the venous Hb oxygen saturation, and PaO_2 is venous oxygen partial pressure.

6.3.2.4 Acute Respiratory Distress Syndrome

ARDS is a condition that causes fluid to occupy the lungs to make oxygen not to reach the other organs. Fluid leaks from small blood vessels collect as tiny air sacs in the lungs to make the blood not to carry enough oxygen to the rest of the body. Organs such as kidneys or brain might not work the way as intended and result in life-threatening ARDS. Oxygen consumption is dependent on oxygen delivery over a wide range of oxygen delivery values in acute respiratory failure. This dependency phenomenon is much stronger in ARDS than in respiratory failure due to other causes. Due to the abnormal dependency of oxygen consumption on oxygen delivery, changes in the oxygenation status may not be reflected by changes in mixed venous oxygen saturation in ARDS. Patients with ARDS on mechanical ventilation with PEEP, oxygen delivery, and oxygen consumption are linearly related except at high levels of oxygen delivery.

With the help of pulse oximeter device, the following attributes are collected and analyzed in edge gateway:

i. ID
ii. Hemoglobin (HGB)
iii. Arterial Hemoglobin Oxygen Saturation (SaO_2)
iv. Venous Hemoglobin Oxygen Saturation (SvO_2)
v. Arterial Oxygen Partial Pressure (PaO_2)
vi. Venous Oxygen Partial Pressure (PvO_2)
vii. Cardiac Output (CO)

The values received from individuals using pulse oximeter are shown in Table 6.1.

In order to ensure the privacy and security of the data, FHE scheme is applied in edge gateway where the data are encrypted homomorphically and used for further analysis. Upon encrypted data, analysis is carried out to detect whether a person has ARDS or not by any number of arbitrary computations. Table 6.2 portrays the encrypted data values collected through pulse oximeter device.

TABLE 6.1

Data Collected via Pulse Oximeter

ID	HGB	SaO_2	SvO_2	PaO_2	PvO_2	CO
1	13	88	66	82	31	8
2	10	91	56	80	27	4
3	16	99	73	79	44	9
4	14	95	73	89	27	7
5	16	95	72	90	37	4
6	17	92	58	84	31	5
7	9	93	58	92	33	5
8	18	95	80	84	36	3
9	9	100	76	82	30	3

6.3.2.5 Analysis in Edge Server

A person is said to have ARDS if following rules are satisfied as explained in Fig. 6.3. The analysis is performed upon encrypted data in edge server by acquiring the real-time value from the patients.

- DO_2 value – less than or equal to 330
- HGB value – less than or equal to 11
- VO_2 value – less than or equal to 240

Table 6.3 presents the analysis carried out in edge server to detect whether a person has ARDS or not.

Fig. 6.4(a) represents output graphically based on DO_2 and Fig. 6.4(b) shows the output based on VO_2. X-axis represents the ARDS patients and Y-axis denotes DO_2/VO_2 values.

Fig. 6.4(c) represents the output graphically based on HGB and Fig. 6.4(d) shows the output based on DO_2, VO_2, and HGB. X-axis represents the ARDS patients and Y-axis denotes HGB value in Fig. 6.4(c).

6.3.3 Case Study II: Blood Pressure Monitor to Predict Hypotension in Edge Server

When the heart beats, it pumps the blood to the whole body that gives energy and oxygen. As the blood moves, it pushes against the sides of the blood vessels. This pushing strength of blood is called blood pressure. Blood pressure is vital as high blood pressure leads to high risk of health problems and low blood pressure results in strain of arteries and heart. The blood pressure parameters are systolic and diastolic. The blood pressure is highest when the heart beats, pumps the blood which is called systolic pressure. When the heart is at rest between the beats, the blood pressure falls which is called diastolic pressure. The normal blood pressure

TABLE 6.2

Encrypted Data Collected via Pulse Oximeter

ID	HGB	SaO$_2$	SvO$_2$	PaO$_2$	PvO$_2$	CO	CaO$_2$	CvO$_2$	DO$_2$	VO$_2$
99530653	26979418	70765932	29657567	13269364	1.21E+08	33735285	78645868	6248914	2.65E+16	2.3E+16
85456837	26957382	25998638	9654469	14646988	1.16E+08	26891249	9632375	24929517	2.59E+15	2.83E+16
33735285	1.02E+08	39124645	9654469	97458792	1.21E+08	6248914	99321270	67911415	6.21E+15	4.27E+15
68319184	26957382	39124645	32820610	25877398	92840941	33735285	77565818	24929517	2.62E+16	2.3E+16
1.05E+08	44723235	1.07E+08	1.16E+08	18195755	82536300	68319184	9632375	67911415	6.58E+15	6.91E+16
6248914	26891249	1.03E+08	1.16E+08	1.07E+08	80828047	68319184	1.18E+08	6248914	8.09E+16	2.3E+16
1.01E+08	99321270	39124645	13269364	18195755	46795202	85456837	45329396	15429419	3.87E+16	2.88E+16
26891249	26891249	53738496	95375810	48966385	85269507	85456837	78645868	26891249	6.72E+16	7.3E+16
26979418	26891249	1.07E+08	1554024	32820610	72540251	68319184	1.18E+08	6248914	8.09E+16	2.3E+16
1.18E+08	1.02E+08	80519520	14250207	73532190	99894387	85456837	44723235	26979418	3.82E+16	5.34E+15
78645868	1.18E+08	72011312	9654469	25877398	67393447	68319184	1.02E+08	26979418	6.96E+16	2.3E+16
67911415	26979418	1.03E+08	1554024	79792123	1E+08	85456837	78645868	1.01E+08	6.72E+16	2.88E+16
1.02E+08	26891249	97458792	92499315	70765932	72540251	85456837	1.18E+08	6248914	1.01E+17	2.88E+16
24929517	1.18E+08	97458792	56273301	62720582	44546924	1.05E+08	67911415	1.18E+08	7.14E+16	1.05E+17
26957382	26891249	97458792	1.03E+08	1.2E+08	80828047	68319184	26979418	1.05E+08	1.84E+16	2.3E+16
44723235	26891249	39124645	1.03E+08	1.2E+08	1.21E+08	1.05E+08	1.18E+08	1.05E+08	1.25E+17	7.18E+16
99321270	67911415	39124645	79891290	9654469	80993363	1.05E+08	26957382	26979418	2.83E+16	1.1E+17
15429419	78645868	1.07E+08	92499315	23695237	99894387	85456837	24929517	26979418	2.13E+16	5.84E+16

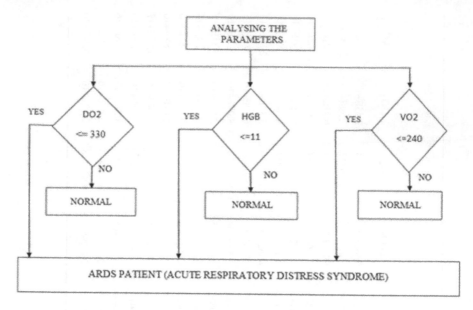

FIGURE 6.3   Parameter analysis.

TABLE 6.3
Outcome of Analysis

ID	DO$_2$	HGB	VO$_2$	ARDS_PATIENT
99530653	2.65E+16	26979418	2.3E+16	Yes
85456837	2.59E+15	26957382	2.83E+16	No
33735285	6.21E+15	1.02E+08	4.27E+15	No
68319184	2.62E+16	26957382	2.3E+16	No
1.05E+08	6.58E+15	44723235	6.91E+16	No
6248914	8.09E+16	26891249	2.3E+16	Yes
1.01E+08	3.87E+16	99321270	2.88E+16	No
26891249	6.72E+16	26891249	7.3E+16	Yes
26979418	8.09E+16	26891249	2.3E+16	Yes
1.18E+08	3.82E+16	1.02E+08	5.34E+15	No
78645868	6.96E+16	1.18E+08	2.3E+16	Yes
67911415	6.72E+16	26979418	2.88E+16	Yes
1.02E+08	1.01E+17	26891249	2.88E+16	Yes
24929517	7.14E+16	1.18E+08	1.05E+17	Yes

range is 120/80 mm Hg where systolic pressure is 120 and diastolic pressure is 80. The systolic pressure is given more attention as it is a factor for cardiovascular disease. Blood pressure is considered as high blood pressure and low blood pressure. If the blood pressure range is 140/90 mm Hg or higher, it is known as high

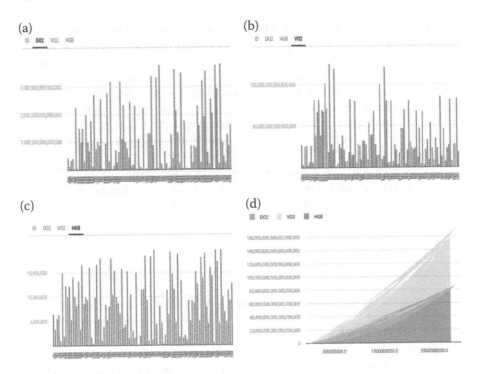

FIGURE 6.4 (a) Graphical output based on DO_2. (b) Graphical output based on VO_2. (c) Graphical output based on HGB. (d) Graphical output based on DO_2, VO_2, and HGB.

blood pressure, whereas the range below 90/60 mm Hg is known as low blood pressure. The systolic and diastolic values help in calculating mean arterial pressure [9]. Mean arterial pressure is the average pressure during a single cardiac cycle. The mean arterial pressure value should be at least 60 mm Hg to provide blood to the organs of the body. If the mean arterial pressure value is less than 55 mm Hg, it is known as hypotension.

Shen et al. proposed a new method to estimate blood pressure continuously based on five parameters extracted from ECH and PPG. These parameters were used to fit the values of systolic blood pressure (SDP), diastolic blood pressure (DBP), and mean arterial pressure. The five parameters considered are PWTT, ecgPeriod, ppgSystolicTime, ppgDiastolicTime, and ppg_K. The stepwise regression is being used for fitting the multiple linear regression equation using SPSS. This method is of great value as this can be used in wearable devices so that it can monitor the blood pressure continuously and send to the edge devices for further analysis [10].

6.3.3.1 Mean Arterial Pressure

Mean arterial pressure is the average blood pressure in a person's blood vessels during a single cardiac cycle. MAP is essential for measuring the pressure necessary for adequate flow of blood to the organs of the body. It is important to have a MAP of at least 60 mm Hg to provide sufficient blood to the coronary arteries, kidneys, and brain. The normal MAP range is between 70 and 100 mm Hg. If the MAP value departs from the range, it provides negative effects on the body. The factors affecting MAP are blood pressure, heart rate, amount of blood pumped out of the heart per minute, resistance to blood flow in the vessels. The high MAP value causes stress on the heart because it works harder than usual to push the pressure in the vessels. The low MAP value leads to shock and in the end death of cells and the organ systems. If the MAP range falls below 55 mm Hg, it is considered as hypotension [9].

The hypotension is known as low blood pressure when the blood pressure reading of systolic falls below 90 mm Hg and diastolic falls below 60 mm Hg [9]. A mean arterial pressure less than 55 mm Hg can cause hypotension. MAP is calculated using the formula:

$$MAP = \frac{SBP + 2(DBP)}{3} \tag{6.5}$$

where SBP is systolic blood pressure and DBP is diastolic blood pressure.

6.3.3.2 Edge Server Analysis on MAP

Using blood pressure monitor device, systolic and diastolic values are collected from the people and are stored in edge server for analysis of hypotension as shown in Table 6.4. To ensure safety, values are homomorphically encrypted and determine whether a person has hypotension or not.

The MAP formula is applied over the encrypted systolic and diastolic blood pressure values. During analysis, the calculated MAP value is compared with the encrypted value of "55". If the calculated MAP value is less than the encrypted value of "55", then the person has hypotension and the result is added to the database in the edge server as shown in Table 6.5.

TABLE 6.4

Data Collected via Blood Pressure Monitor

ID	Gender	Systolic_Pressure	Diastolic_Pressure
1	M	36	23
2	F	38	39
3	M	37	35
4	M	26	33
5	F	4	17
6	F	12	31
7	M	59	19
8	F	8	35
9	M	39	70

TABLE 6.5
Identification of Hypotension Based on MAP

ID	Gender	Systolic Blood Pressure	Diastolic Blood Pressure	MAP	Hypotension
664817	664767	664866	664826	664839	No Hypotension
386811	386760	386909	386859	386875	No Hypotension
323231	323180	323328	323278	323294	Hypotension
377916	377863	377997	377952	377967	No Hypotension
201409	201355	201484	201444	201457	No Hypotension
345325	345271	345394	345359	345370	No Hypotension
568918	568862	568951	568921	568931	No Hypotension
641068	641011	641130	641090	641103	Hypotension
155601	155544	155682	155632	155648	No Hypotension

6.3.4 CASE STUDY III: BODY COMPOSITION SCALE TO DETECT HEAT INDEX IN EDGE SERVER

Physical fitness is more important to be considered in day-to-day life. Body compositions such as weight, height, BMI, body fat, lean mass, humidity, and indoor temperature are to be calculated to maintain a healthy life. Body composition scale is a measuring scale that is used to measure body compositions using bio-impedance method. Bio-impedance is the common method used by household scales to calculate body composition. This device uses the bio-impedance method by using four conductors to determine the hindrance of electrical flow through the body, and uses that to calculate the total body water. From the total body water, it estimates nine data points. The nine data points that are measured by this device are weight, BMI, body fat, body water, lean mass, bone mass, muscle mass, visceral fat intake, and daily calorie intake. This device has a separate sensor for indoor temperature and humidity, so the thermostat can be adjusted to keep the body in optimal condition. The measured humidity and indoor temperature values are transmitted to the edge server for analysis/processing of data. Humidity and indoor temperature are used to measure heat index that may range from 27°C to 57°C. An increase in humidity and indoor temperature leads to an increase in heat index that results in health problems such as fatigue, heat cramps, heat exhaustion, and heat stroke. These health effects may vary according to the heat index range. The heat index is calculated by the relative fractional proportion of humidity and indoor temperature.

Borga et al. proposed a brief overview of common non-invasive techniques for body composition assessment method based on fat-referenced quantitative MRI. For whole-body measurements of adipose tissue (AT) or fat and lean tissue (LT), DXA and quantitative MRIs are comparative with respective linear correlations. But the agreement was found significantly lower for visceral adipose tissue [11]. Bos et al. proposed two models for predictive analysis in health care as Cox Proportional Hazard Model and Logistic Regression Model. They proposed FHE scheme for the standard way of encrypting data bitwise. The functions of these regression models can be approximated by polynomial expressions in integer values. The advantage of this approach is that a single ciphertext contains much more information than just a single bit of plaintext [12].

6.3.4.1 Heat Index

Heat index is defined as the amount of heat consumed or measured in the surrounding area. Heat index is calculated with relative humidity and indoor temperature that is measured either in Celsius or Fahrenheit [13]. The heat index is calculated to identify the damage of excessive heat in human body. The formula used for calculating heat index in Celsius is:

$$HI = c_1 + c_2T + c_3H + c_4T\ H + c_5T^2 + c_6H^2 + c_7T^2H + c_8T\ H^2 + c_9T^2H^2$$

$$(6.6)$$

where
  HI – heat index (°C),
  T – temperature (°C),
  H – humidity (%),
  $c_1 = -8.78469475556$,
  $c_2 = 1.61139411$,
  $c_3 = 2.33854883889$,
  $c_4 = -0.14611605$,
  $c_5 = -0.012308094$,
  $c_6 = -0.0164248277778$,
  $c_7 = 0.002211732$,
  $c_8 = 0.00072546$,
  $c_9 = -0.000003582$

The heat index may range from 26°C to 54°C and above. The heat index gradually increases with the increase in temperature (°C) and humidity (%). The heat index is directly proportional to temperature and humidity and increases within a particular range of temperature and humidity. The causes and effects of various heat index are shown in Table 6.6. An extreme range of heat index may lead to many

TABLE 6.6

Causes and Effects of Heat Index

Celsius	Causes	Effects
26–32°C	Caution	Fatigue – Tiredness, anemia, arthritis, chances of heart failure
32–41°C	Extreme caution	Heat cramps – Painful muscle cramps, cramps in abdomen, arms, and calves
41–54°C	Danger	Heat exhaustion – Dehydration, chances of obesity
Over 54°C	Extreme danger	Heat stroke – Chance of chronic heart disorders

health problems such as fatigue, heat exhaustion, heat cramps, heat stroke, and death, as well as increases pre-existing chronic conditions such as various respiratory, cerebral, and cardiovascular diseases.

6.3.4.2 Heat Index Analysis in Edge Server

The attributes collected from the device are shown in Table 6.7. Out of the attributes collected, humidity and indoor temperature values are considered in this case study to analyze the heat index value of an individual. The computed heat index value is added for future reference and to send notification to the individual from the edge server. Finally, the required values based on the dependency transmitted to cloud server.

The relation between humidity and indoor temperature is shown in Fig. 6.5.

TABLE 6.7

Data Collected via Body Composition Scale

ID	Gender	Weight	Lean Mass	Height	Age	BMI	Humidity	Indoor Temp
1	11	96	66	174	23	32	40	27
2	11	87	67	189	22	24	55	28
3	3	110	67	185	22	32	78	30
4	3	104	70	195	26	27	62	29
5	11	61	45	149	24	37	46	32
6	11	104	74	189	24	29	56	33
7	11	92	57	147	26	43	99	42
8	11	111	67	154	25	47	100	31
9	11	90	64	174	25	30	72	33
10	3	103	58	169	23	36	40	23

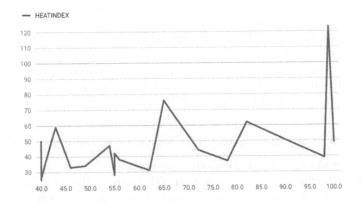

FIGURE 6.5 Humidity vs. indoor temperature.

TABLE 6.8
Encrypted Data in Edge Server

Gender	Weight	Lean Mass	Height	Age	BMI	Humidity	Indoor Temp
8759977	6078807	3401121	9785855	4991836	2004675	11128148	2483337
8759977	5502958	7028914	5236734	12452562	2861229	12913267	11207314
7287978	489574	7028914	11121095	12452562	2004675	8464926	4376414
7287978	8641303	8364146	2494302	4423197	2483337	3494691	4783100
8759977	2965637	9674157	3106086	2861229	2483337	12341017	2004675
8759977	8641303	3761029	5236734	2861229	4783100	9515812	2825248
8759977	3491122	6435069	1443346	4423197	755833	2875700	11941524
8759977	9425892	7028914	12506679	9602157	7619130	5294229	2411361
8759977	11570875	2220647	9785855	9602157	4376414	2155873	2825248
7287978	2483413	9159513	5826950	4991836	2893632	11128148	4991836
8759977	9933321	3401121	2494302	4423197	10807818	11311722	11941524
7287978	3829416	12502933	8720536	2483337	2004675	12913267	12243833
7287978	4963122	1288510	6791505	2004675	2483337	9692189	2893632
8759977	12351819	755833	374451	4376414	10807818	5481331	3926546
8759977	10624327	2220647	9127255	12243833	12452562	6654600	2004675
7287978	5736913	12351819	7205351	12243833	12341017	3689073	4783100
7287978	489574	5481331	5841334	8475679	9674157	11128148	7813470
8759977	7608372	11761603	10386854	2004675	1817539	11941524	11128148
8759977	5294229	8464926	10001765	11207314	7619131	755833	755833

The homomorphically encrypted value of the attributes is shown in Table 6.8 to guarantee privacy and security.

Heat index is computed and is analyzed in edge server and effects are included in edge server database for further processing/notifications as shown in Table 6.9. The causes are categorized as caution, extreme caution, danger, or extreme danger based on the range of heat index. Also, the severity leads to many health problems such as fatigue, heat exhaustion, heat cramps, and heat stroke.

Total time taken for analysis by different FHE schemes in edge server is measured in nanoseconds (ns) and is presented in Fig. 6.6.

The case studies considered show the process of acquisition, storage, and processing (computation) of information effectively in edge server. Secure storage and processing are guaranteed by applying FHE schemes.

6.3.5   USE CASE - EDGE COMPUTING/ANALYTICS IN INDUSTRIAL IOT

Mr. T. Viswanathan, CTO, Maxbyte Technologies

Maxbyte Technologies is an Industrial IOT Products (IIOT) & Solutions company for the manufacturing companies in various industries such as automotive, aerospace and defence, industrial products, consumer products, and process

TABLE 6.9
Heat Index Effects in Edge Server Database

Humidity	Indoor Temp	Heat Index	Heat Index Range	Effects
11128148	2483337	4423197	caution	fatigue
12913267	11207314	11207314	caution	fatigue
8464926	4376414	3926546	extreme caution	heat cramps
3494691	4783100	2411361	caution	fatigue
12341017	2004675	2825248	extreme caution	heat cramps
9515812	2825248	6845336	extreme caution	heat cramps
2875700	11941524	11380161	danger	heat stroke
5294229	2411361	6654600	danger	heat exhaustion
2155873	2825248	1817539	danger	heat exhaustion
11128148	4991836	9602157	caution	fatigue
11311722	11941524	9137937	danger	heat stroke
12913267	12243833	11941524	danger	heat exhaustion
9692189	2893632	3494691	danger	heat stroke
5481331	3926546	7619130	danger	heat exhaustion
6654600	2004675	8475679	extreme caution	heat cramps
3689073	4783100	262766	extreme caution	heat cramps
11128148	7813470	7687514	danger	heat exhaustion
11941524	11128148	6654600	danger	heat exhaustion
755833	755833	3077204	danger	heat stroke

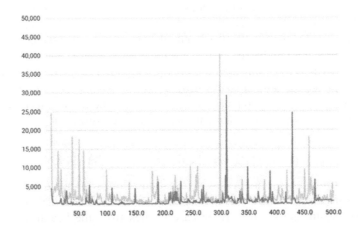

FIGURE 6.6 Total time taken in nanoseconds.

industries. Maxbyte provides end-to-end Industrial IOT Products & Solutions from sensors to analytics. Edge computing/analytics plays an important role in acquire raw data from the assets and sensors, processes and shares the required information to the IIOT enterprise applications.

There are various use cases on edge computing/analytics applicable in Industrial IOT from basic data collection to high-speed data processing in use cases such as vibration analytics. The specific use case to be described below is vibration-based predictive analytics for manufacturing shop floor machines.

The objective of this use case is to predict the machine failure in advance based on the vibration measurement and take corrective and preventive measures to avoid machine downtime. In the existing scenario, the machines failures are identified only after the issue has occurred on the machine and the maintenance team takes the required corrective action to correct the issues. This generally is an expensive process since the machine is already into breakdown which impacts the production, and the cost of repair/recovery is high.

Solution to the above-mentioned problem is identifying the machine failure in advance and take the necessary corrective and preventive measures to avoid the complete machine failure. Machine vibration analytics helps in identifying the machine failures effectively. To do this, the vibration sensors are mounted on the critical parts of the machines and the vibration data are acquired at 10/20 KHz sampling rate. The acquired data need to be processed at the edge device to identify various frequency components in the measured vibration signal and identify any anomalies.

To predict the machine failures, the historical data of the previous machine failures and the associated critical machine parameters including vibration play a crucial role. Based on the historical data, the diagnostics and machine failure model has been created and deployed in the IIOT enterprise application in production. Based on the real-time data captured and the processed data on the edge device, the predictive model deployed on the server predicts the machine failures in advance, and the necessary alerts and notifications along with the recommended action to be taken will be sent to the respective maintenance users. Based on this information, the maintenance engineer takes the required corrective and preventive actions to resolve the problem in advance.

The primary benefit of this use case is the elimination of the high cost of repair/ recovery from the machine breakdown which not only impacts machine health but also the production. The incremental improvements done on the machine will also ensure higher machine uptime and enhanced machine utilization.

6.4 CONCLUSION AND OPEN RESEARCH CHALLENGES

Edge computing propels use cases across multi-domains including autonomous vehicles, smart cities, industrial automation, gaming, content delivery, financial sector, and healthcare sectors. Three case studies from the healthcare sector are considered and a detailed illustration is elaborated in this chapter by ensuring the proper acquisition of data, secure storage, and dynamic onboard processing. To assure secure storage homomorphic encryption schemes are applied and analysis is performed upon the encrypted data to safeguard the framework against invasive attack vectors. The case studies enlighten the secure compute and processing capacity of edge gateway/server for real-time applications. Edge in conjunction with advanced analytics algorithms supports real-time models and control in various sectors. However, the open challenge for researchers/developers is to understand the security and processing requirements of the applications as they differ from sector to sector while enabling edge computing systems.

REFERENCES

1. Tseng, M., Edmunds, T., & Canaran, L. (2018).*Introduction to edge computing in IIoT: An industrial Internet consortium white paper*. Edge Computing Task Group.
2. Whitaker, B. E. (2018). Cloud edge computing – beyond the data center. *OpenStack White Paper*, 1–8.
3. Anitha Kumari, K., Ananyaa, M., Keshini, P. S., & Indusha, M. (2020). Prediction of heart disease using LDL in edge computing systems. In *Proc. 26th (Virtual) Annual International Conference on Advanced Computing and Communications (ADCOM 2020)*, NIT Silchar, India, December 16–18, 2020.
4. Gentry, C., & Halevi, S. (2011). Implementing gentry's fully homomorphic encryption scheme. In *Proc. Annual International Conference on the Theory and Applications of Cryptographic Techniques (EUROCRYPT 2011)*, 129–148.
5. Dijk, M., Gentry, C., Halevi, S., & Vaikuntanathan, V. (2010). Fully homomorphic encryption over the integers. In Gilbert H. (ed) *Advances in Cryptology – EUROCRYPT 2010. EUROCRYPT 2010. Lecture Notes in Computer Science* (Vol. 6110). Berlin, Heidelberg: Springer. 10.1007/978-3-642-13190-5_2.
6. Wu, S., & Weidong, Y. (2009). A medicare system of wireless sensor networks. In *Proc. 2009 9th International Conference on Electronic Measurement &*, 3-53–3-57, 10.1109/ICEMI.2009.5274240.
7. Kenneth Roberts, J., Disselkamp, M., & Yataco, A. C. (2015). Oxygen delivery in septic shock. *Annals ATS*, *12*(6), 952–955.
8. Mc Lellan, S. A., & Walsh, T. S. (2004). Oxygen delivery and haemoglobin. *Continuing Education in Anaesthesia Critical Care & Pain*, *4*(4), 123–126.
9. Kendale, S., Kulkarni, P., Rosenberg, A. D., & Wang, J. (2018). Supervised machine learning predictive analytics for prediction of postinduction hypotension. *Anesthesiology*, *129*(4), 675–688.
10. Shen, Z., Miao, F., Meng, Q., & Li, Y. (2015). Cuffless and continuous blood pressure estimation based on multiple regression analysis. In *Proc. 2015 5th International Conference on Information Science and Technology (ICIST)*, Changsha, China, 117–120, 10.1109/ICIST.2015.7288952.
11. Borga, M., West, J., Bell, J. D., Harvey, N. C., Romu, T., Heymsfield, S. B., & Leinhard, O. D. (2018). Advanced body composition assessment: From body mass index to body composition profiling. *Journal of Investigative Medicine*, *66*(5), 1–9.
12. Bos, J. W., Lauter, K., & Naehrig, M. (2014). Private predictive analysis on encrypted medical data. *Journal of Biomedical Informatics*, *50*, 234–243.
13. Brooke, A. G., Bell, M. L., & Peng, R. D. (2013). Methods to calculate the heat index as an exposure metric in environmental health research. *Environmental Health Perspectives*, *126*(10), 1111–1119.

Index